Choosing End of Life Nursing

Text copyright © 2016 remains with the authors and for the collection with ATF Press. All rights reserved. Except for any fair dealing permitted under the Copyright Act, no part of the publication may be reproduced by any means without prior permission. In- quiries should be made in the first instance with the publisher.

Ethics:
Volume 3, Number 1, 2016

Ethics: Contemporary Perspectives
We live in an evolving and increasingly complex global community and with this complexity comes a broad range of ethical issues. The new interdisciplinary journal, Ethics: Contemporary Perspectives, seeks to bring together scholars from across the humanities, social sciences, and sciences, including disciplines as diverse as philosophy, law, medicine and the study of world religions, to discuss these broad ethical issues in contemporary society. A peer reviewed journal, Ethics aimed at exploring our complex world, addressing both old and new ethical issues through scholarly discourse.

This is a new, international, interdisciplinary, and refereed journal which is to be published annually by ATF Press in association with the University of Adelaide Research Unit for the Study of Society, Law and Religion (RUSSLR). The publication is both an on- line and print edition journal. The first issue of the journal has an international line up of leading scholars in a range of disciplines from the USA, Canada, New Zealand, France and Australia. It will address the theme of 'The Ethics of Ethics' and will come out in the first half of 2013. The second edition in 2014 will deal with 'Space Ethics'.

Editor Board
Dr Bernadette Richards, Law School University of Adelaide, Editor in Chief.
Associate Professor Paul Babie, Director, Research Unit for the Study of Society, Law and Religion, University of Adelaide
Professor Robert Crotty, former Director, Ethics Centre of South Australia, Emeritus Professor of Religion and Education, University of South Australia

Business Manager
Mr Hilary Regan, Publisher, ATF Theology, PO Box 504 Hindmarsh, SA 5007, Australia. Fax +61 8 82235643.

Vol 3/ 1 2016

Subscription rates
Print: Local: Individual Aus $55, Institutions Aus $65.
                                   Overseas: Individuals US $60, Institutions US $65.
OnLine: Local: Individuals Aus $45, Institutions: Aus $55.
                                   Overseas: Individuals US $50, Institutions US $60
Print and Online   Local: Individuals Aus $65, Institutions Aus $85.
                                   Overseas: Individuals US $70, Institutions US $80.

Ethics: Contemporary Perspectives is published by ATF Press an imprint of the ATF Press Publishing Group which is owned by ATF (Australia) Ltd (ABN 90 116 359 963) and is published once a year. ISSN 2201-3563

Cover design by Astrid Sengkey. Text Minion Pro Size 11

Choosing End of Life Nursing

by Susan Bardy

Adelaide
2016

Abstract

Death is inevitable—none of us will escape it. Ending life with a terminal illness is a slow and rather lonely process. I am interested in the question of why some nurses choose to work in the field of palliative care. I am one who willingly stepped into the role of being with patients at their most vulnerable time—when death became inevitable.

My nursing history has spanned fifty years, of which the last twenty were in palliative care of terminally ill and dying patients. What was it that influenced me to move from a curing model to comfort caring only?

My work is an account of how I discovered palliative care nursing after thirty years in the acute-care setting. I migrated to Australia at the age of seventeen after the violence of World War II and the death of my father in a refugee camp. It seemed that taking on nursing was the best way to settle into a new life. I was happy with general nursing but had a feeling that there was more I could contribute to my patient care. My mother's unexpected death with cancer was responsible for showing the way. She died in the hospice unit of the hospital where I was employed. Sitting by her side showed me another aspect of nursing that attracted me to a career change. I transferred to the Hospice after mother died and remained there for twenty years. Naturally I wondered why this change of direction happened.

Acute care of patients taught me much about nursing but did not satisfy my wish to give effective personalised patient care. Hospice nursing was different. Working in the hospice I learnt to embrace notions of clinical competence, a sense of calling, compassion, empathy, and comfort with death and personal mortality.

Table of Contents

Introduction
Prologue

'Do something more with the rest of my life'	1
A new beginning	4
A little girl's dream	4
A letter to my son	5
A map to follow my journey	8

Section One: This Is How It All Began

1. Death of Apu – my Father: Almost a lifetime ago	12
Broken life threads – December 1944, Budapest	15
Apu – the first man I loved	16
Too young to understand	16
I did not know this was going to be Apu's last day	17
Looking back: Looking forward	20
2. My mother is dying: the change to my professional thinking	21
Beginning of the end	22
Comfort and peace – *Anyu* in the hospice	24
Rest as the final gift	25
What does this tell me?	27
Postscript	28
3. Death of my life's partner	29
Entering a twilight zone	29
What now?	30
Coping	33
The end	35
The family together	37
The funeral	37
What has this taught me?	38
Face to face with death again	39
4. Afterthought	39

Section Two: My Way Of Getting There

5. Writing that marries personal experience with transformation	42
Auto-ethnography	42
Auto-ethnographic Researcher	46
Jessica and I	50
Parting thoughts	53
6. Partnership of narrative and knowledge	54
Doreen's story	54
Remember where you are	57
7. Power of knowledge – Patterns of knowing	58
The received view	59
Perceived view	59
Interpretive view	61
8. Consciousness: the patient and the nurse's knowledge building	63
As it happened for me	66
Nursing: a vocation that transforms	66
Caring as natural ability	67
Shirley	72
Vocation: does it promote transformation?	75
9. Hospice and palliative care: a historical review	77
10. Palliative care: the ideology and practice	78
Pioneers of note	80
Dame Cicely Saunders – Britain	80
Dr Elizabeth Kubler-Ross – United States of America	81
Dr Balfour-Mount – Canada	82
Dr Colin Murray-Parks	83
These four leaders	83
The World Health Organisation (WHO)	84
Hospice and palliative care world-wide: a brief overview	85
My palliative care	86
Pain that suddenly changes	87
One night in the hospice	90
Bibliography	93

Prologue

'Do I do something more with the rest of my life?'

It is 11 o'clock at night. At last I am on my way home. Slowly closing the back door of the hospice behind me I look ahead on the way to the car park. I sigh deeply as I walk faster in the cold night air. I have just finished an afternoon shift that was anything but smooth sailing. The shift was complex: there was pain to be eased; two wives had to be consoled (their husbands had died and their children all were wide-eyed and looking very scared); the phone did not stop ringing, and I did not have time for a bite to eat all shift. Come to think of it, neither was there any tine to go to the bathroom during the eight hours of work. As I get into the car and turn the engine on, the radio comes to life. I turn up the volume to keep myself awake until I get home. I am just so tired! My mind is so full of other people's problems that I know I will take them to bed with me, and in less than eight hours time I will be back to face it all again. As the car gets closer to my home I ask myself: 'Should I be doing this?' As I arrive at the front gate, I am reminded that I need to open the garage door. This is a worry; I cannot remember how I actually got home at all along those dark roads. Entering the cold house I head for the shower and a glass of my favourite red wine, hoping to try and put myself into a dreamless sleep.

Five hours later and it feels as if my head had only just hit the pillow. The radio wakes me with a Bach cantata; far too slow. The Radetzki march would be more appropriate. It is five o'clock on a dark winter's morning. I have no choice but to get up and get ready for another day at the hospice. At my time of life getting up in the early hours of the morning is a real chore, a problem. I cannot jump out of bed. I am tired and feel that the years are catching up with my aching body. A quick breakfast, a cup of coffee and I should be ready to face the day.

Arriving at the hospice, I stop the engine and remember to switch off the headlights. I quickly get out into the cold and dark morning. On my right the buildings loom dark. The wind and rain sting my face.

Shivering, I jog to get out of the harsh winter weather.

I do not feel like working today. There should really be a law against two shift separated by only a few hours sleep: an afternoon shift followed by a morning shift.

Another busy day greets me as I open the back door of the hospice. Call bells are ringing, footsteps tread the carpet and the door to the sluice room noisily shuts as someone comes in or goes out with a bed pan. Staff who have worked all night look tired. They must have been busy, but they still have energy to greet me and give me a warm hug. I am in my professional home in the warm comfort of being welcomed not only as a colleague but also as a friend.

This morning is no different from any other start to a day's work. Those of us who have arrived for the morning shift mumble brief 'good mornings' to each other after getting and then sipping on hot coffee or tea and as we head for the room where we will get the 'hand-over' from the night staff. In that room we will listen to the disembodied voices of the night staff on a tape-recorded. It is often difficult to hear what they are saying on the tape recorder because it has recorded so many other shifts over time and the tape is worn out and should be replaced with a new one. Under a new 'efficiency drive' handovers between all shifts must be fast and to the point, hence no face-to-face encounter with each other but just a recording by one group of staff to the next shift. There is no time for debriefing about how the shift has played out.

As we listen, we wonder if any one died in the small hours of the previous shift.

I am restless as I sit on the edge of the chair. I ask myself do I really want to be here again today. Yes I do, this is my life and I would be lost without it. I briefly glance at the list of patient's names: a series of admission dates, diagnoses and, yes, ages. Involuntarily my eyes focus on the age of those in the beds they will never get out of; the beds that are now their final home before the end. I stare at the numbers in that column and shiver. Again eight out of sixteen patients are younger than I am. What does this mean?

Do I need to be told that I have overstayed my welcome? The tape recorded handover washes over me. I am not listening to the nurses speaking on the tape recorder any longer. Instead I am hearing another message which is being sent by those in the beds in the hospice: 'Do something more with the rest of your life. Look at me. I had so much I wanted to do and now it is too late.'

I heard a voice telling me this time and time again in my active nursing career but never listened seriously to it. Why does it intrude again, and right now? I am being urged to wake up before it is too late, before the energy runs out and before I am the one in the bed that I would never get out of. I need to take heed of this list at seven o'clock in the morning when it shouts at me: 'Once again there are eight dying people in the beds whom you have out-lived.'

Coming from the tape recorder, I catch the voice of one of my colleagues, let us call her Diana, but barely can I hear her softly spoken words as she talks of yet another night shift full of its specific needs and problems. The voices in my head do not let me go; they keep reminding me of something that I do not want to hear: 'time waits for no one'.

I am confused. Should I leave this work or should I stay? Should I leave and go out into the world and see if I can make a difference with something out there? Does anybody out there want or need me?

From the moment the recorded messages started at barely 7am I can not help but think about the future. On any other morning I would listen to the handover, and be ready to go, but following the stressful shift of the night before, which is now seemingly only just a few hours ago, I yield to other thoughts which I normally would block out. The human voices on the tape recorder wash over me but the voiceless messages coming from the patients in their beds in the hospice keep on troubling me.

They gate crash my mind telling me to review the rest of my life. I have to pay attention because these other messages are now for once so intrusive. In fact soon after this day I acted upon their advice and resign from my position as a registered nurse in the hospice. A month or so later I say farewell to my colleagues and work at the hospice and walk out the back door for the very last time. It was not easy thing to do. My footsteps sounded hollow, I did not dare to turn around. Eyes staring ahead I could hardly make out the shape of the car because I was crying. It was hard to stop; windscreen wipers do not clean away tears that come from many years of an active professional life. I just sat in the car and once I felt safe to drive I switched on the engine and drove home.

Such was the beginning of what most people would call the beginning of a 'happy retirement'.

I was a free spirit; I could do whatever I wanted to do with my time.

Yes, there was no need to get up at 5 am any longer, but I still did. There was this feeling of uselessness and loss of purpose. Giving up a career after fifty years leaves a feeling of emptiness that could easily swallow up any possible ideas of future ambitions. Fortunately I was resilient enough to look for alternatives and remembered what sent me into retirement. The day I started listening to my body, and the messages coming from dying people who were younger than myself, was a significant one. Both my body and those messages told me not to waste the years I still had ahead. So I began a journey of looking at my work as a registered nurse in a hospice.

My goal

My intention in writing of this is be one of a storyteller, so that the readers will sense the passion behind the words. I have gone back and examined stories and reflections, referred to the thoughts and discussions of others, and reflected on it all. I have tried to make this clear in my writing when I include my personal stories, poems and journal entries.

A little girl's dream

A brief childhood memory introduces my early passion for caring and healing.

Many years ago in another land there lived a six-year-old girl who was fascinated by sickness and healing. She watched as doctors and nurses did magic things to make her better in the hospital she visited often. She was scared when she could not breathe but felt safe with the doctors and nurses. This little girl wanted nothing more than to become one of the angels who looked after her. She decided that she would learn to be a doctor. I was that little girl who years later grew up to be a nurse.

I would like to continue in this free flowing manner, but as a clinician I lack skills in the art of story telling. Nurses generally produce reports of the patient's medical condition with dry and scientific language that focuses on medical matters. Whenever I addressed emotional problems in patient records my colleagues let me know that I should not expect anybody to read long-winded passages on irrelevant matters. There was never enough time for reading anything but doctors' orders. My chosen methodology for the study prescribes deep and emotionally meaningful involvement. To be true to this I had to find the best way to introduce my work. Suddenly it occurred to me that writing in the form of a letter to someone I value, and who understands me, would be the way to get around this problem. I am certain that Alex, my son, a consultant physician and cancer specialist would be interested in my plan to research an interdependent specialty. Thus, here to begin this story, is my letter to Alex.

A letter to my son

Good Morning Alex,

You may wonder why I write instead of use the phone. I do not blame you since this is the first time we have exchanged ideas in writing. This letter serves a double purpose. One is to explain why I have been a virtual hermit for a long time; not seeing you as often as I would have liked to. Second is to clarify what I have been involved in during the time we rarely met. I hope that after reading this letter you will come to understand why I feel the need to talk of my career in nursing, since you were a part of my life and are a physician. Coming to the time in my life when I thought I had done it all and begun a quiet retirement, I suddenly had an insatiable urge to do one more thing.

You already know that I left active clinical nursing sometime ago but I do not think you knew that I never stopped believing that I could still contribute to my profession in some way. That is why I decided to become a student once more. I am taking a stroll to scrutinise my life's work that started with informal caring, developed into general nursing and ended in palliative care. I mainly focus on the last twenty years that were spent in hospice nursing because what intrigues me is the fact that I never really knew why I switched to end of life nursing after a thirty-year career in general patient care.

You may well ask what I call experience? I will give you a philosophical answer. Every moment in every day brings new situations seldom evaluated or explored in detail on the spot. Yet on reflection experience often is identified as a teaching tool that can enable knowledge that may benchmark future activities. In other words the benchmarks or standards are guidelines arrived at through experience. The German philosopher Hans Georg Gadamer's elegant explanation is to the point when he says that experience is not static, it is expectant and is ready for the next encounter with a new situation. The one who is involved in an experience is 'particularly well equipped to have [another] new experience to learn from'.[1] *Alex, retirement gave me an opportunity to reflect on my career and alerted me to how the twenty years in hospice nursing rounded up my professional work appropriately. End of life caring of patients enabled my complete devotion to patients, and provided the reason to create this study that speaks of my move from a clinical career into the world of the new challenge of palliative care research.*

Let me tell you about the day when it all came together.

I came to the realisation one day that I have reached one of life's crossroads and acknowledged that at seventy-three I would have to step aside and allow a younger and fresher generation of nurses to take over. Up till that morning I was undecided about retirement. But that day looking at the age column on the patient list, for once gave me the impetus to leave the hospice, ending my active nursing life. It was a difficult choice but I had to make it. I was ill at ease at the time and

---

1. H Gadamer *Truth and Method* (New York: Continuum Publishing Company, 2000), 335.

could not explain why. Stepping down from constant giving to a life of uneasy 'leisure' was overwhelming. I was certain that I could still contribute to nursing in some way. The end of clinical work need not mean that my involvement with palliative care had to end. A feeling that my work was not yet completed gradually overtook the restlessness of retirement. I felt a drive to explore the what, why and how of palliative nursing. The truth of the matter though was that I had no idea where to start. With encouragement by a nurse colleague, I applied for and was accepted into a PhD program. Suddenly I had a chance to be involved with a research project to investigate nurses' transformation on the way to becoming palliative carers. I was not sure if I was ready for it though. The world of clinical nursing did not prepare me. It was a lot easier to comfort a patient in pain, calculate a morphine dose or face the anger of grieving relatives than to argue points of theory.

Alex, planning for my research future reminded me of preparing for the countless marathon runs I successfully completed. A higher university degree, just like the marathon, is hard work. It involves a lot of 'training' and constant focus on the goal. I wanted to create a narrative project around the perception of my transformation from the principles of 'curing', to simply giving all round 'comfort care', while adopting the standards of palliative nursing to a research method. Let me explain what I mean.

Over the years I have noticed a change in my nursing values. I gradually began focusing less on the 'saving lives' model as I followed a more holistic caring ideal that dealt with the body, mind and spirit of the patient. I sensed that there was more to nursing than being in busy wards with short term admissions where patients improved rapidly and the nurse was driven to concentrate on medical matters only. I wanted an opportunity to spend more time with people who had serious illness and needed management of emotional problems beside their physical state. That is why I adopted Sabatino's perspective that 'care as sensitivity to the vulnerability of persons'[2] as my mantra. I wanted to be truly present with patients and knew that I had to 'slow down' and take more time to listen or go along the path of being with patients and physically care for them.

---

2. CJ Sabatino 'Reflections On The Meaning Of Care', in *Nursing Ethics*, 6/5 (1999): 574–582, 574.

I had observed palliative care work for some years as a clinician. I had also developed an interest in the nurse as an individually distinctive being not just as one who works out of a 'textbook'. That is when I looked at myself as the hospice nurse and wondered what had impacted on my caring ideals to such an extent that I had transformed into a different class of patient manager, carer, nurse. While asking why I chose palliative care it became obvious to me that influences were multiple and significant.

This study begins with introspective personal narratives. It explores my entry in to the field of nursing and the beginning of my vocational metamorphosis from being involved in 'curing' to being a palliative nurse who was 'caring'. I present my life through 'a wide angled lens to get a feeling for the ethnographic influence' and then return inward 'to my vulnerable resistant self' to construct the research framing.[3] I tell stories of grief and suffering in my own life that theorises my palliative care.

Well, Alex, this out-lines in brief what I have been spending so much time on recently.

With all my love

Mum

A map to follow my journey

Broadly speaking, personal transformation is at the heart of this writing. A need to understand that transformation is what has led me to explore my experience and to think more deeply about the shifts that have occurred with time. Simply put, the intention of the study is to tell the story of the change in my nursing care delivery that I now understand was started by my experience of family bereavements.

The methodology I have used is auto-ethnography[4] which has supported me in working on multiple levels of consciousness. It

---

3. C Ellis *The Ethnographic I* (Walnut Creek, Lanham, New York, Oxford: Alta Mira Press, 2004). 37.
4. Broadly stated auto-ethnography *is an evocative style of writing and research based on narrating experience that prefers showing to telling. It combines voices of the*

recommended using a 'wide angled lens' to be ethnographic and then go inward to the self to produce narratives of personal experience. This in itself was another form of transformation, one associated with the research experience. Once started, this kept on evolving, never to return to the same starting point.[5] My study recounted my life experiences through vignettes, it informed my understanding of palliative care nursing and gave me a picture of the transformative process from a focus on 'curing' to one of 'end of life caring'.

Section One—*This is how it all began*—focuses on close family deaths that give the background for my vocational identity that over time transformed my caring dimensions and sanctioned a diversely developing nursing role. This is where embodied knowledge of loss and grief endorsed the auto-ethnographic blending of the 'personal' with the 'cultural'.

Section Two—*My way of getting there*—encompasses the methodological and theoretical discussions in five sections. The first deals with the methodology of autoethnographic research as it reflects on palliative care nursing expanding on and including transformation as espoused by nursing theorists Newman[6] and Parse.[7] The second emphasises the partnership of narrative and scholarship that looks at nursing knowledge and the therapeutic relationship of caring. The third introduces nursing as a vocation that transforms and discusses experience as a theory. The fourth includes a personal perspective, while the fifth brings in key players of palliative caring, debates historical, theoretical and philosophical aspects.

---

personal and the other in interactive communication making the study therefore a narrative inquiry. For more on this see C Ellis, The Ethnographic I (Walnut Creek, Lanham, New York, Oxford: Alta Mira Press, 2004).
5. J Mezirow, *Transformative Dimensions of Learning* (San Francisco Jossey-Bass, 1991).
6. M Newman, *Health as Expanding Consciousness,* second edition (Sudbury: Jones and Bartlet Publishers, 1994).
7. RR Parse, editor, *Illuminations: The Human Becoming Theory In Practice And Research* (Subury: Jones and Bartlett Publishers, 1999); RR Parse 'The Pattern That Connects', in *Advances in Nursing Science,* 24/3 (2002): 1–7.

Section One

This is how it all began

This study is essentially an exploration of nursing transformation; it contains a number of my personal stories, interspersed with tales of others who walked with me in that journey. The question I ask points at the directional change in a career that digressed from healing to easing the life course of dying people. This happened to me past my mid-life, a time when people start thinking of retirement. I became focused on a possibility of changing and transferring to an area of nursing where sick patients are actually looked after the way that I thought that they should be—with gentle giving care that centres mainly on comfort and rest.

A lot happened before my ideological transformation. The full story ought to be told, otherwise to explain the 'why' of my personal change would be difficult.

It all started when I decided to use a research methodology that prescribed or allowed me to be not only ethnographic but also autobiographical. To write a study that consists of personal experience in a culture is not as easy as I first thought it would be. The only easy part was when I decided to ask myself why I find comfort and privilege in nursing dying people. Trying to find the answer to these things was when the difficult part started. It took some time, and endless thinking, to eventually get the message that the explanation should begin with telling where I came from. There was a need to go back in time and find possible signposts that could indicate why I decided on a nursing career in the first place, and then opting for palliative care later in life. I asked myself if personal life events could have influenced a professional coming of age. Once it became clear that this was the way to do it, I could not stop writing.

The following three introspective narratives tell of experience in my immediate family that I maintain could be responsible for shaping my life. They mirror significant events that deeply influenced the development of my personality. I talk of three deaths in my immediate family that I consider to have impacted on my professional integrity. In the Prologue I mentioned the early years when I was a child who was often ill. While that is only a briefly put observation, it is of some importance to pre-empt the way my life evolved as it did. That is why now I go back to another time in another country where existence became difficult for a child but more so for an intelligent teenager trying to make sense of the destruction of human lives.

The first story in this trilogy gives a picture of the birth of a commitment to people in need. This is where I begin explaining the roots of my caring ideals. I purposely begin in early childhood because I want to emphasise the importance of how that has had an influence on my later emotional development. I write the first part mainly as a reflective adult because some of the story of the six year old self came from my mother. But as the story evolves I have vivid memories of the fifteen year old 'I' and will tell the story in the first person.

1. Death of Apu—my father: almost a lifetime ago

From four years of age I was often in the hands of doctors and had frequent hospital visits to treat severe asthma attacks. My earliest memories were that of gasping for breath in my mother's lap where I felt safe. I spent more time in bed with frequent bouts of pneumonia than playing with my siblings. My school days are full of blurred memories of being sent home consistently because I was so sick. What I remember clearly though was the fervent desire to go to school. There were times when I denied feeling ill just so that my mother would allow me to go with my sisters. Unfortunately she was a sharp observer and often I did not go to school with them. A tutor and my mother then took over the task of educating me at home where I developed a passion for reading. I will always remember how my mother taught me to write. She had inexhaustible patience with me;

a child who rather read a book than practice writing skills. I must admit this remained a part of me for the rest of my life. I still prefer reading to writing.

There were some things in early childhood I clearly remember even now. Christmas in the year of 1939 is one such memory. The evening of 24 December is an important date in a wintery Europe, because that is when the baby Jesus delivers all the presents. My sisters and I would remain in the playroom all day to wait for the Christmas bell that would signal the arrival of the Christ child.

I was sick with a bad cough that Christmas Eve in 1939. It was really cold outside. It had been snowing all day. We were restless, it was still hours till evening but we could hardly contain ourselves and invariably squabbled. I shivered and shut my eyes between coughing spasms. I knew what would come next, an asthma attack. Tears rolled down my face, the handkerchief that I could not do without; a ball in my sweaty hands. Why is this happening? I asked myself. I would love to go to school and chase the ball without that wretched jumper I always had to wear. I am sick of hearing mother and grandmother calling: 'Zsuzsi, hol van a kotott kabat' [where is your jumper?]. I wished I could lose it one day! It did not really matter how I was dressed because I always got sick sooner than later whether I was wearing it or not.

It was getting dark outside. We were told to dress in our best clothes, and be on our best behaviour. Then it happened, the ringing of the Christmas bell called us to watch father open the tall white double doors of the dining room. 'Wow'. On the grand piano stood the most beautiful Christmas tree I had ever seen. I forgot the cough and the wheezing and sang carols with my sisters before opening the presents. It turned out to be a good day after all.

By eleven pm we were more than ready for bed. After a restless night I woke to see my mother's anxious face. I remember her ringing the hospital and calling an ambulance. Paramedics could not drive up to the house. My father had to dig a path in the snow so that I could be carried out of the house and to the ambulance. I cried quietly between wheezy breaths. I so wanted to stay at home. My presents 'Baby Jesus' brought the night before were under the Christmas tree waiting for me. None of my protestations worked. I was bundled into the ambulance and taken to the hospital. My mother sat with me on the way. Arriving at our destination I was deposited into a small bed in a large room full of other sick children. Mother was not allowed to stay and that began six weeks of feeling abandoned. Women in long black dresses looked after me, and I eventually got to know that they were called 'sisters'. It was a first time meeting with the women in long black dresses who rarely smiled and disappeared for long periods warning us to be good, because they were going to chapel to pray for us. There were only short visits by mum and dad and I got a lot sicker before eventually getting better.

I gradually discovered that it was not all that bad, that at times the hospital could be interesting. The sisters often let me help the other children and that made me feel special. There were times when I was allowed to parade with a stethoscope around my neck and other times I watched breathlessly as the doctors gave injections. I got to like that hospital even if at times I felt homesick. When I got better and went home I quietly played with my dolls and I was the doctor.

My second visit that winter was to the infectious diseases hospital where I barely escaped from having an operation. My ears got so bad that I went completely deaf and the doctor was going to dig a hole in my head to get out the pus. The situation was intriguing. I took it all in quietly. That time mother stayed with me. I was not scared at all.

In later years there were more hospital visits. My tonsils were removed among other problems and that was when I really made up my mind to become a doctor. I was eleven years old, a child who was never well enough to play. I loved reading and observed things around me constantly. My childhood consisted of being sick, going to the doctor, lots of injections, having hospital visits and putting up with the dreaded icy cold chest compresses when pneumonia nearly killed me several times.

I was far too serious as a child—not having much fun—and not asking a lot of questions. But I was hell bent on becoming a doctor; that was my future aspiration. I did not see nursing as an option. Being a doctor was more interesting because they helped me the most whenever I was sick, at least that is how I saw it at the time. I wanted to be just like them. A few years later I headed down a different path, dictated by the unexpected.

Broken life threads—December 1944, Budapest

This was the year when World War II saw my home-land, Hungary, invaded by Russian troops. The war crept towards the capital. Budapest was not only battered by constant air raids but before Christmas 1944 the enemy became entrenched in the outer suburbs, judging by the not so distant artillery fire.

I remember well the noise of guns firing and wondered how far they could be from home. Initially I wasn't scared because my parents did not look worried. However, by the time I was eleven years old I suffered emotional and cultural pain. Our family with thousands of others, fled to Western Europe to escape being killed by the enemy. Our parents tried to shield us the best they could. We were bombed, shot at, starved and went without any comforts of life. We saw people badly wounded as families pulled off the road.

This was in April 1945.

The war came to an end a few weeks later, just as we arrived in the Austrian countryside. We were no longer hunted but hunger became our enemy while we lived on a train for some months.

The refugee camp where we eventually landed seemed like heaven after having lived on that train we called home from April to August that year. Life by then was relatively quiet, there were no air raids and we were no longer shot at. Camp life gave us a roof over our head and we had some food. We lived in a two roomed wooden hut and father got work in the nearby coalmine. For three years he worked there in a job he was not trained for. I remember him as a quiet uncomplaining man who always had a kind word for us. Unfortunately he got sick in December 1948. He had an operation on his left leg to remove a lump and was sent home after a short stay in hospital. A few weeks later I noticed a gradual change in him. He got thinner, could not return to work and became very quiet, but never complained. Every now and then his face looked different. It looked as if he could be in pain. I was fifteen by then and wanted to ask questions because I did not understand what was going on, but no one seemed interested in answering me. I knew he was sick, but did not know how bad it really was.

Apu—the first man I loved

Yes Apu was desperately ill, but I did not know that he would die soon. At that point I had no idea he would be the first dead person in my life. The situation was more heartbreaking because of the circumstances surrounding it. He did not die in a hospital between white sheets, doctors and nurses watching every nuance of his suffering. He closed his eyes for the last time that April day in the year of 1948 in a European refugee camp. We lived in that camp without running water and without a bathroom. Our family of six was crammed into two small rooms that served as living, sleeping and cooking quarters. It was there that my father's life came to an end without pain relieving drugs or even a comfortable bed. As a fifteen year old girl I experienced the worst thing any child could dream of experiencing—the death of a parent.

Too young to understand

It is Palm Sunday, I woke up and through the small window I saw the sun and the blue sky. I was always the first up but today was different, it was earlier than other mornings, I could not sleep for reasons I cannot explain. Sitting bolt upright I looked around the place we called home and asked myself why are *Anyu* (Mum) and *Apu* (Dad) not waking up yet. Sitting here with my feet planted on the floor I suddenly remembered another Palm Sunday three years before when on the road we nearly got killed by the low flying Russian planes strafing our column of fleeing refugees. *Apu* and I walked ahead of the ox-cart that held what was left of our possessions and where the rest of the family were sleeping. I was so very scared then as I was again now, but for a different reason. Today I was worried about *Apu*, he had not been himself since he had had an operation nearly four months ago. I cannot understand why he was taking so long to get better. He had changed a lot lately; he barely talked to us and looked so very thin. His clothes no longer fitted him; the trousers needed a belt to hold them up.

I had though at the time that he had left the hospital too soon after the operation. However, he had not liked it there and it was by then nearly Christmas any way.

'I am feeling much better, it is good to be here with you all. I will not go back to that cold place ever again', he said smiling on that freezing December day. To make certain that we believed him he tore to shreds the letter he brought home without reading it. None of us ever knew what it was in the letter.

Now in April *Apu* was far from well.

He was never one to complain but lately he had mentioned headaches that hang around. Daily visits to the local doctor made him feel worse instead of easing the headache. I noticed the unusual way he was walking, only shuffling slowly but he insisted on going it alone. I still had lots of questions but did not ask them. *Anyu* would not have told me anyway. She would have considered me too young to understand.

I did not know this was going to be Apu's last day

A little later in the quiet of the morning I sensed movement in the next bed and saw *Apu* slowly trying to stand up. Swaying, he was hanging on to the furniture on the way to the small stove in the next room. I watched him silently. He needed several attempts before he succeeded in lighting the small stove. *Apu* always had coffee and a cigarette first thing in the morning. This time the pot he put on the stove is empty and there is no coffee in the cup he takes back to bed. I took the empty saucepan from the fire before it completely burnt out and turn off the heat.

Back in bed *Apu* rested his head on the one threadbare pillow, and tried to light a cigarette. This also looked like a difficult task and he put the burning end into his mouth. I expect him to feel the pain but there was no response. Reaching out I removed the cigarette from his mouth, but he did not even notice it.

He picked up the newspaper and starts to read it upside down.

'What is this, why is he so strange?' I asked myself. *Apu* has never been like this. There is something different about his eyes as he looked at me. Both his left and right eye are in the middle looking at his nose. I shiver as I looked at him and wished there was someone I could ask to tell me what was going on. As if an answer to my silent plea *Gitta*, *Ildi*, [my sisters] *Anyu* and even *Nagymama* [grandmother], who also lived with us, woke up and I ask them to have a look at *Apu*.

He reacts to the movement around him by opening his eyes and he tried to speak but we could not understand a word. '*Apu* is your head hurting?' I asked. He shook his head as an answer. His face was red, his eyes were now closed bulging behind the lids almost tearing them and his breathing was difficult to listen to. It sounded as if he could not get enough air into his lungs. I have had asthma since I was four years old so I knew all about bad breathing. Standing there with every breath he took being painful I go over to him. It hurts as I can hardly breathe myself.

That was when *Anyu* asks *Gitta* and I to get dressed and went for the doctor from the village. We both welcomed the opportunity to get out into the warm fresh air and partly run, partly walk to get there quicker. The doctor is not home and his wife tells us he will not be able to come even when he gets back. He is busy now with a new baby and afterwards he has to be at the Sunday football match as he is the team's doctor. We start crying. What will happen next?

We decided that we must go home and tell *Anyu* that there is no one to help us.

Getting back to the camp we find *Apu* in a worse state, if that is possible. Our sobs become stronger as we knelt down by his bed. *Anyu* hugged us all, something she does not do often, so there was a certain indication that this was serious, *Apu* must be really sick. I, as the eldest of the children, somehow felt the burden of helplessness most. I sense that something should be done to help him but have no idea what.

In the afternoon *Hortens* an old friend knocked on the door. She has no family so she is a frequent visitor, we do not like her because she takes up a lot of *Anyu*'s time and does not like children. Today, however we welcomed her, as she is the only one to offer help. *Hortens* insisted on going down to the village and if need be to drag the doctor back with her, but she came back alone.

By now *Apu* is not responding to us at all no matter how insistent we are with our questions. Eyes closed his breathing is loud, full of bubbles, and the colour of his face turns from red to purple. I prayed that this should stop, not realising what I was asking for. Eventually deep down I knew something serious is going on, that he must be dying. Not knowing much about death I only imagined that this could only have the one ending as I repeat to myself: 'Stop, and if you need to, please die'. None of us expected help anymore from anyone.

Apu's breathing little by little slowed down. Eyes behind his lids bulged even more. His face was that of a stranger. The spittle on his lips was something I had never seen before. I had never seen my father spit. He no longer moves: he just sleeps. The sun goes down. It is getting dark.

Standing at the foot of the bed I could only hear the moist bubbly sound of *Apu*'s breath that was gradually slowing down. Moving closer to the head I soon noticed the stillness of his chest as I watched it stop moving altogether, I held my breath and listened.

There is no sound anymore. Did this mean he will never talk to me again? I could not believe that I felt so much relief to see him peaceful at last even if it meant that he could be dead.

The rest of the family and *Hortense* came closer. No one cried. There was only relief as *Apu*'s face becomes pale and calm. There is a knock at the door and *Nagymama* let in the doctor. He dashes to *Apu*'s bed, and stands not believing what he sees. He then tells us of the letter in his files from the hospital that outlined the seriousness of *Apu*'s illness, and of the need for further treatment. *Apu* had ignored that letter. That is when I remembered the letter that *Apu* tore to pieces at Christmas time. Surely that had been a copy of the one sent to the doctor. I should have stopped *Apu* destroying it. *Anyu* tried to assure the doctor that there was nothing any one could have done to change the situation at that late stage. While that is true I still wondered how she forgot so soon that *Apu*'s painful end could have been eased maybe with some medication. The doctor leaves and we are at last alone.

The hours that follow were quite eerie. My family are Roman Catholic tradition, yet none of us thought of calling a priest. The doctor organised the undertakers and they sent ahead two priests, and *Anyu* by that time realised our omission about the last rites of the Catholic Church and asked the priests to administer them. Their refusal came without hesitation: 'We cannot do that because he has been dead too long and his spirit is gone, we can not give him the holy oils. We will pray with him though.' They both then knelt down and recited words in Latin. I did not understand any of this as I looked at the two kneeling figures. I was only confused because I could not make sense of statement that 'the spirit has gone'. To me *Apu* was still here. I was upset that he was not treated with some dignity even if he could not talk to us any more. He was still *Apu*.

The undertakers came, we watched in silence as *Apu* left us.

Then we went to bed.

As hard as we tried, sleep did not come. The silence of the wooden building was disturbed by loud creaking noises. This sometimes happened in the summer but never on a cool spring night. *Anyu* tried to find an answer but she could only say: '*Nem akar bennunket itt hagyni*' (He [*Apu*] does not want to leave us). This reminded me of what the priests had said about the spirit long gone. No holy oils. I did not believe that *Apu*'s spirit had left us. We had been through so much together. He would not just leave without letting us know what that meant to him.

Apu's spirit remained with us, even if only for this night.

Looking back—looking forward

The story of my father's death in that refugee camp in Austria describes a crucial experience that I saw later as shaping my approach to life. My introduction to death could not have been any more traumatic as I was old enough to understand the implications of ending a life in silent agony.

Writing this story after more than half a century of not remembering, initially made the visualisation of those events rather difficult. Suppressing the memory must have been a sub-conscious act to forget and go on living. But the process of researching life events and the transformation of nursing priorities prompted me to remember. Scrutinising my ongoing professional aims I recognise how the lived experience in the dark days of the refugee camp could have been responsible for the formation of the caring ideals I developed and carried with me ever since the death of my father. The vision of myself as a young woman standing at the bedside listening to the movement of air in and out of a struggling chest, grappling with helplessness and fright, was real. Now with my adult eyes I can see how my adolescent self must have suffered while trying to make sense of the tragedy of my father's death. I am well able to understand now how that emotional struggle could have led to making a subconscious decision to become a carer. At that stage my youthful immaturity did not know what shape the future would take. However, later, when I eventually made sense of the meaning of my father's agony, I knew that I wanted to learn how to help others who suffer like him.

In 1951 when I was seventeen, my family migrated to Australia bringing about many life changes. To learn a new language and fit into a different culture were the immediate tasks, but I also had the challenge of training to be a nurse. This posed a few problems but after completing five years study I achieved my goal of graduating as a nursing sister, as the nursing qualification was known in 1956. That was the beginning of a career that left me with much to be thankful for.

The loss of my mother with cancer came many years later. It was under better circumstances but, nonetheless, for me it was still a painful experience

2. My mother is dying: the change to my professional thinking

The period between the deaths of my parents brought many changes. Those years saw me get married, bear and raise two sons and develop a successful nursing career. Juggling family and work did not ever present a problem. I learnt to be two people where one never interfered with the other. Beside work and family commitments, I found that the care of my aging mother became an added responsibility. I accepted that; I owed her a debt for being the sole parent and provider at a crucial time of my existence. She was independent to a fault so much so that it was difficult to know if she had any health problems. It was a shock when she got sick. Without being aware, mother looked after me even in death by helping me to write the final chapter of my nursing career.

Anyu was a frail eighty-year-old the day she collapsed. She had had a tough life. Widowed when aged fifty in a European refugee camp made her responsible for rearing three teenage daughters, an awesome task at the best of times. We did not appreciate the full implications of that until becoming mothers of teenagers ourselves. *Anyu* as the sole provider had the task to migrate to the other side of the world and provide a new life for the family. She worked hard at various jobs and was healthy until her early seventies when a mild heart attack slowed her down. But I never dreamt the implications of the ovarian cancer that reared its ugly head ten years later. She never mentioned any discomfort or pain that must have been a part of the disease ravaging her body. The end to her suffering came rapidly after the diagnosis.

Beginning of the end

The phone rang just as I shut the front door to go shopping. I decided to answer it and heard the anxious voice of *Anyu*'s neighbour Mara: 'Susan, I heard Mary call out five minutes ago, something she has never done before and I found her on the floor. She must have slipped while pulling on her stockings. After putting her on the bed I thought it is best to call you.'

I thanked her and hung up. While jumping into the car my head was spinning, I thought about the woman who would live forever. '*Anyu* cannot be sick, she cannot collapse,' I said to myself, 'she is indestructible!'

I found her in a poor state. Her speech was slurred as she tried to tell me what had happened.

One look at her convinced me that she might have had a stroke. Her mouth was crooked and she could only move one arm. I rang her doctor who suggested admission to a private hospital. I quickly knocked that idea on the head. Having watched *Anyu* for sometime I feel that her doctor was missing some aspect of her health which should be investigated. I had noticed of late that she had lost weight and was only picking at her food. I was concerned; she needed a thorough physical check-up that only a large public hospital could provide. The nurse in me imagined the worst.

Anyu's doctor eventually appeared. He organised an ambulance and arranged for her admission at the nearest public hospital. As usual he was in a hurry, just as well because I was in a mood to lecture him on the way mother was neglected even as he visited her each week. Writing prescriptions for new drugs was what he did best. While waiting I packed her toiletries, nightgowns and her medications. My mind was racing as I was convinced that this was something serious. *Anyu* was resting on her pillow, her eyes darted from corner to corner around the small apartment, I think she was saying goodbye to her little rented home. The two paramedics who arrived handled her gently as she disappeared into the back of the ambulance. I followed them in my car telling myself to calm down. In the hospital emergency department a young medical intern took *Anyu* under his wing and asked a lot of questions, some which I could not answer. Fortunately *Anyu* by this time managed to fill in the blanks. Eventually she was taken to a ward and into a clean fresh bed. I felt at peace with her care. There was now the promise of a thorough investigation of all of her health issues that had, in my view, so far neglected for some time. *Anyu* was weak and tired so I decided to leave soon as she closed her eyes and went to sleep.

The following day my patients in the hospital where I worked had no idea how distressed I was. *Anyu* had a scan soon after admission and when later I phoned the ward to find out about the result I was told to make an appointment with her physician, the nurses could or would not tell me much. I was certain this could only mean one thing; Ayu had serious problems. I often gave the same reply when asked about test results for my patients or their relatives. The golden rule is that the nurse does not disclose a diagnosis or any other significant health information, as that is the doctor's prerogative.

The appointment with *Anyu*'s physician was the next day.

I had it all worked out. Should she have a life limiting diagnosis I would only ask for comfort care. *Anyu* must not have any invasive treatment; she would not be artificially kept alive. If things were as bad as I thought, then she needed to have peace at the end of her life. Luckily, when I met the physician, he gently told me that the problem is an aggressive ovarian cancer. He suggested that because of her age and frail condition the best thing is to have comfort care only. I felt relieved.

The physician took over the role of the decision maker that can so often be difficult one for a daughter to be. He gently hugged me and saw me to the door. Going up to the ward, each step reinforced the sadness that had now overcame me. What was I going to say to *Anyu*? I should not have worried. The nurses told me that she knows the test results; she had already been told. Sitting by her bed, stroking her hand and before I had a chance to say anything she said: 'I know I have a tumour, but it is all right.' That instant I realised that she was aware of her imminent death, and in her characteristic stoic way she was letting me know that she does not want to talk about it. She did not speak of dying then or later.

Next day when on duty in the surgical ward where I worked I met one of the pastoral care nuns who sensed my distress: 'How are things Susan?' she asked. I broke down and told her the whole story of my mother's illness and prognosis. She hugged me and took over. 'I will go and see your mother', she assured me. She not only visited *Anyu* but also informed me that she had organised a transfer to the hospice unit that is a part of the hospital. *Anyu* would be in the same building where I was working.

I had no idea what a hospice was. All my nursing work was in healing and life saving, any other area was a mystery to me. This was the first time any one talked about end of life comfort in a hospital. I was always under the impression that all people must at least be offered a cure. *Anyu* died in that hospice ten days later.

Comfort and peace—*Anyu* in the hospice

Her transfer was arranged for the following day. When I visited her there for the first time I was a little anxious. At the front door a kindly middle-aged nun warmly welcomed me. The hospice was in an old building and had an aura of peace and quiet as if the cares of the world were left outside the ancient walls. I suddenly felt 'special'. It was the most amazing nursing environment I had ever been in. *Anyu* had peace and comfort. Her pain was controlled, and her spiritual wellbeing was also being taken care of. She had come home, and I felt I had as well.

I spent a great deal of my free time with *Anyu* over the next ten days. I watched her get weaker, and witnessed her slowly die before me. *Anyu* and I have similar physical features. When I saw her losing her grip on life I came face to face with my dying self. My body is my mother's body. I sensed in some way how it must feel when one is dying.

The pastoral care nun often visited and we sat and prayed together. We had a go at saying the rosary and I could not remember the words of the 'Hail Mary' in the two languages I speak fluently. Movement of visitors at the next bed came to the rescue.

'There is too much noise here, we cannot pray properly', is all she could say. I was glad to be saved from an embarrassing situation. *Anyu* slept through it all.

Spiritual care is important in a hospice under the care of the Catholic Church. Daily Holy Communion is offered to those who are Catholics and want to receive it. The Sacrament of the Sick, as the last rites are known these days, is an additional bonus. When the priest came for the anointing ceremony I remained with *Anyu*. She looked up and smiled. But I will never forget my reaction of absolute horror as he asked her: 'Would you tell me your sins.'

This was devastating! Does it matter whether she 'sinned' or not? 'She is dying for God's sake father', I thought to myself. Her life was a constant battle and she more than paid for her sins. She deserved a smooth ride to that other world, wherever that may be.

I could not forgive the priest for making *Anyu*'s final journey that little bit more arduous. Still that priest at least treated her with respect, not like the ones after *Apu*'s death where the priests denied him a spiritual ending, of receiving an annointing on theological grounds.

Rest as the final gift

I sat with *Anyu* and hoped that I could be there when she took her last breaths. One day there was a change in her. She slept most of the time. There was only the occasional smile when she opened her eyes and looked at me. There was not much talk between us.

Nurses patiently, quietly attended to her comfort. The injections and other medications that she was given to control her pain were done with a minimum of fuss. She was washed and massaged with soothing lotions and her mouth was gently moistened with iced water.

I loved witnessing her presence in the bed and welcomed the comfort she received; she deserved all of this so much. This was when I remembered *Anyu* as the woman who sold her wedding ring to buy food for her children. I recalled her as the mother who was at my sick bed so many times as I grew up. I still remembered that *Anyu* was the one who patiently taught me how to read and write. I was blessed by having that time for remembering all of these and other things in our life together as mother and daughter.

My husband insisted that I come home to eat and have some rest. No way did I want to leave, I had a feeling that she would die that night. Still I believed she could wait until the next day, which was the 21st of November. That date was special for her; it was my father's birthday and was their wedding anniversary. But, I had to go home and have some rest

Between two tall trees my little old car sat forlornly. I got into the driver's seat, put the key in the ignition, started the engine and I slowly crashed into the tree in front of me. There was no way I could drive home now. My husband had to come in and he drove me home. I had something to eat and go to bed. I tossed and turned all night and had very little sleep. My mind was with mother. I was so disappointed that I could not be with her. Probably it was meant to be. The next day I found out that both of my parents were watching over me when my car slowly hit that tree. When it was finally towed away the mechanic found that the braking system had completely failed. How lucky was I that the crash did not happen on the way home!

At seven in the morning the phone rang. I picked up the receiver; it was one of the nurses from the hospice: 'Susan, I am so sorry but your mother died at 1 am. Have you chosen a funeral director?'

I could not think. I was angry with my husband for stopping my returning to the hospice the night before. I did not want to speak to him and only stammered the name of an undertaker to the nurse. Standing there motionless I hung up the phone. That is when I remember that *Anyu* and *Apu* were together on their special day; she died at one o'clock on the morning of the 21st of November. After a strong coffee I was calm and headed back to the hospice.

I will never forget the warmth of the Mother Superior when I get there. That was the first time I felt the caring support of complete strangers. The funeral was a quiet affair with only a few people attending. Nurses who cared for mother were present, and that is when I decided that working with these special people would be a privilege. That was more than twenty years ago. I joined the hospice team six months after mother died and remained there until my retirement.

What does this tell me?

The more I think about my mother's death, the more I am convinced, that while sitting at her bedside I had a transforming experience. It did not happen the first day but it crept up on me gradually over the ten days she was in the hospice. Day after day soaking up the hospice environment, I wondered how it was possible to feel so peaceful in the face of tragedy? Watching the nurses busily yet quietly going about their task, I wanted some answers. The questions were intimate and impacted on the way I saw nursing care after visiting the hospice as a health care recipient. At the time of my mother's death I was involved as a care provider of surgical patients who were expected to get better. There I was constantly planning for the patients' return home as the wounds healed, the appetite improved and pain vanished. It was always joyful and positive.

Oddly enough, being with a close relative who was dying I did not feel the opposite. I was not depressed or sad. I was at peace and confident. On reflection I realised that behind these emotions was the reality that both *Anyu* and I were cared for. That is what mattered, and that is what countermanded other negative feelings. The nurses supported me in coping with the death environment in that hospice at my mother's side. Unconsciously they were modelling a caring approach that encouraged my wish to be just like them and work with them. Sitting with mother gave me the opportunity to closely pay attention and absorb the effect that the environment had on my outlook concerning caring ideals. Sitting quietly with mother influenced my transformation. There was the chance to be vigilant and pay close attention to nurses managing my mother's care. They never sent me away, but included me in the moment out of respect for the time that may be too short for being a daughter. There were several existentially important elements in this that now looking back remind me of O'Hara's discussion of Carl Rogers' message regarding personal transformation that is a '… simple and widely shared human capacity for empathy, genuineness, respect for the other and faith in people's competence for growth, [that] can be relied [on] to bring about transformative effects in relationships.'[1] This made sense to me

---

1. O'Hara, M 2002, 'Cultivating Consciousness: Carl R Rogers's Person-Centered Group Process As Transformative Androgogy', in *Journal of Transformative*

after experiencing first hand a nursing environment where I observed genuinely open empathic respect for not only my mother but also for me. I was touched by the trust, kindness and embodiment of transformed vocational principles. Nurses in the hospice provided end of life care and they did it well.

Postscript

My mother's death was an experience that changed my ideals of care and caring for people needing more than physical symptom management, though I accept and believe that without bodily comfort emotional issues are difficult to handle well. This gives me confidence in my belief that nurses who want to engage in palliative care need a good solid background of clinical knowledge and a well-balanced personality that is gained through extended life experience. I am convinced that the gentle unhurried nursing care of my mother's final days largely influenced the transformation of my approach from curing to comfort caring. However I already had attributes of intuitiveness, intensive caring and a strong interest in people's human values, and accepted as true that commitment to a task is an '. . . ability to believe in truth, importance, and interest value of what [I am] doing, and the willingness to exercise influence or control in the personal and social situations with which [I am] involved'.[2] I know that I have what it takes to be involved in the care for patients at the end of life. For me the importance of addressing emotional and existential problems predominate the body-only-management when there is a life limiting diagnosis. I maintain that health carers should look at the person with a terminal illness as having an extended consciousness to live their life while preparing to die.[3] I found a caring home for my nursing expertise in the hospice that became the last career transformation after some thirty years in nursing.

Hospice nursing became my vocation, teacher, friend, and was where I wanted to end my working days. Little did I realise that

---

Education, vol.1/1 (2002): 64–79, 64.
2. C Kobasa, 'Stressful life events, personality and health: an inquiry into hardiness', in *Journal of Personal & Social Psychology*, 37 (1979): 34–37.
3. M Newman, *Health As Expanding Consciousness*, second edition (Sudbury: Jones and Bartlet Publishers, 1994), 208.

experience of death and dying in my immediate family had a final offering. My sons by now were busy professionals. Alex married with four sons and Richard an international law practitioner had their own lives to live. It all seemed peaceful. Getting towards my long service vacation meant that I could spend more quality time with my husband.

That was not to be.

3. Death of my life's partner

By the time death and dying in my personal life plays out its final act I should have been more than prepared for what is to come. By now I was an experienced hospice nurse with a good knowledge of symptom control and had good grief and loss management skills. I was easily able to recognise existential issues in patients that are other than physical distress. I was sensitive to the human being behind the tortured façade of a disintegrating body. Yet I was not ready for the impact of seeing my husband become a virtual skeleton in only six months following a mind shattering diagnosis of terminal cancer. We were both numb; we could not believe this was happening to us.

Entering a twilight zone

I suspected for some time that Steven was not well. He was pale, had been losing weight, was eating small meals and the wine he always liked was now left untouched. This is what concerned me most because he used to enjoy a nice drop of red at the end of a busy day. Initially I did not connect this all other than to hard work. He was busy redecorating a rental property we owned, getting it ready for the next tenant.

In our thirty-seven year marriage Steven was seldom sick, a headache, a cold occasionally, but nothing more serious. It surprised me when I discovered the antacid tablets in his car. I always maintained that he had a stomach that would digest a rusty nail and any discomfort there would be was unusual and out of place. Steven never talked about his health. He was the true stoic European male and kept things close to his chest. When I asked him about the tablets in his car he admitted to having indigestion that he had had for sometime. 'Steven, is the pain any less since taking that medication?' I ask. 'No, I feel really bad', he replied.

This was quite an admission from one who was always ready with an evasive but 'smart' reply. What really surprised me though was the acceptance of my suggestion to visit his doctor. It was too optimistic to think that he would agree to my presence so I reluctantly suggested the specialist he should ask to be referred to which he actually agreed with. The following week Steven had the first investigation directed at his stomach, without finding anything of consequence. He relaxed but I was really concerned as my nursing instinct told me otherwise. Most of his pain and nausea pointed to something sinister. He continued to lose weight at an amazing rate, becoming weak, and was no longer able to work on the rental property. 'What is happening to this strong man?' I asked myself.

I did not take no for an answer and joined him for the next doctor's appointment. Steven did not ask enough questions. We discuss the CT (Computerised Tomographic) scan results and are told that there is nothing that should give us concern or anxiety. I am not happy. I have lived with and known him for over thirty years. I knew every nuance of his personality and his body. Something was wrong; I sensed it and demanded further investigations because by now I had formed an idea of the diagnosis that is anything but pleasant. Confronting the specialist by phone I suggested he should concentrate on Steven's pancreas. He fobbed me off for being an alarmist.

What now?

Both our sons were overseas and I did not want to worry them until there was a definite diagnosis. Unfortunately the specialist physician independently decided to ring Alex in Canada and tell him that his mother has 'taken it into her head' that his father has cancer. I was devastated! How could he do this without asking first for my permission? This then started off a series of questions by Alex who is also a physician. He is angry with me for not telling him about the problem, and does not accept my explanation of wanting to spare him until there is something certain to talk about. He makes me promise to keep him updated about developments.

I was trying to be calm. I did not want to worry Steven unnecessarily. He was not asking much but I realised that he was confused and anxious. For the first time since I had known him he could not work out what is going on. His sharp intellect usually managed to find an answer for most things. Medical knowledge was not his forte and he relied on the doctors this time, but felt let down by them. To be truthful, I was also disappointed in the physician treating Steven; he was not, in my view, seeing the full picture. A number of other tests he ordered did not come up with any answers either. By now I was not only frustrated but also angry, especially when he suggested treating a possible depression. My answer was to say to 'over my dead body'. I demanded the only diagnostic procedure relevant to the pancreas.

Thank God that test was the next day. I was on leave from work so I would be with Steven for the whole procedure.

Driving to the hospital where the procedure would take place created a level of unease in me. I hoped they would treat Steven well, give pain relief and let him rest as much as possible. But mostly what I was hoping for was an answer to the puzzle of pain, vomiting and weight loss. We were greeted by smiling nurses. They suggested that I should go away for a while because the procedure would take sometime, and it was best if I do something to occupy my mind. The hours pass slowly.

Countless cups of coffee later I returned to the hospital and found the surgeon sitting with Steven. He beckons me to join them, and quietly, gently he explained that Steven had a complex pancreatic tumour and will need an operation. He did not promise a good outcome. While the news was distressing, at last we had an answer for the weeks of uncertainty.

It was Christmas in a few days. The operation was planned for early January. We decided to do our best to cope until then. Christmas would be a quiet one. We celebrated on Christmas Eve, a European tradition when we exchange presents and usually go to midnight Mass. This year we stayed at home and went to bed early.

I returned to work on Christmas day. It felt strange that now I was also a close relative of a cancer sufferer. My mind was still mostly numb but found that understanding for fellow cancer families came more easily. My colleagues were sensitive to the situation and offered help should I need it with day-to-day problems of a newly diagnosed cancer. I admitted that without their compassionate understanding I would find coping a lot more difficult.

On the third day of January I drove Steven to the large public hospital where he was admitted the night before the operation. He carried his bag as he walked with unswerving steps to the private room that will house him for the night. He most probably would be in the intensive care unit by the time I would see him the next day. We hug and I wished him well, promising that I would be back the next day.

At work in the hospice the next morning, I was on edge. I attended to my patients as best I could but my thoughts drifted to the operating room at that other hospital, wondering whether Steven would need to be in the intensive care unit or not after the surgery. What would the surgeon find? Like an answer to my silent question as I walked past the front desk the ward clerk, the one who answers the phone in the hospice. stirred me out of my thoughts and said: 'Sue, the surgeon wants to speak to you.'

'Oh God, this is too soon, the operation should take hours.' While taking a deep breath I looked down at my shaking hands and picked up the phone.

'Mrs Bardy, your husband's operation was a simple procedure. I could not do more than just have a look. I believe you diagnosed this months ago. He has cancer of the pancreas that has spread to his liver and all the abdominal organs. I suggest palliative care may be the best way to go. He can be transferred to the hospital where you work and be cared for by the physicians there. Comfort care is the only thing we can offer now.'

A quiet 'thank you' is all I could say as I hung up the phone.

Standing at the desk I was too shattered and weak to move. It felt so good when a colleague gently put her arms around me. She sits me down in the nearest chair. That is when I lose it and cried uncontrollably.

'Why does cancer take so many people who are dear to me?' I asked. 'What now, please God, what now?' Sobs continued to shake me. I felt so empty and lonely even as nurse colleagues come up with coffee and kind words. Eventually calming down a thought occurs that the operation could have been much more invasive and for no good reason. I looked down my nurses' uniform and remembered that I am at work and have responsibility for patients who, like Steven, are terminally ill. The nurse in me was grateful that the surgeon is a humane person, and admits that Steven is better off having palliative care now because he cannot do anything further to help. Having suspected this outcome for sometime, the wife in me still hoped for more than the three months of life predicted.

Visiting Steven later that day was not easy or pleasant. He was angry at the world, the operation and terminal cancer. He barely spoke to me, and what he said was curt and unkind. He used words that I put out of my mind because they hurt too much. I only stay for a short time; Steven does not want me there. One of the nurses made me a coffee and invites me to sit for a while before driving home.

Arriving home the house loomed dark and empty, the nurse's uniform by now hung creased and limp on my tired body. Turning on the lights in every room did not alter the dark shadows in my mind. All I wanted to do was to go to bed and try to sleep. Yet it was important that I spoke to our sons and told them about their father's operation. I cry as I talked while trying to come to terms with being alone. They both attempted to reassure me that they are with me in thought, but tears slowly keep flowing. I decided that I would think about the future tomorrow, as I could not face another thing then and there.

Coping

Steven came home. He still lost his cool every now and then and I almost lost mine at times. 'Some palliative care nurse you are!' Steven said angrily once. 'I am your wife, not your nurse', I replied but knew that this was only partly true as I was indeed both and sensed that I would need the knowledge gained through nursing to eventually cope as a wife.

Slowly we became resigned to the fact that we would part company sooner rather than later. The cancer that ravages Steven's body was untreatable and was fast growing. The best we could hope for was comfort in spite of the terminal diagnosis. I was determined that Steven would get the 'best' palliative care, but when I suggested to him that I take some time off work he became angry. He did not want to be reminded of how sick he really was. So work for me was just as it was before his illness. I tried to sit back and wait to see if it would be three months just as the surgeon had predicted?

Steven gradually calmed down, was less angry and I wondered how much of the fear of death he kept close to himself. 'Am I the nurse again?' I asked myself. 'Is this OK?'

I was often confused; Steven needed quality life even as that life slowly was fading away. We became closer. For the first time he accepted my help in so many ways. His armour of independence began to exhibit a few cracks. I made decisions about mundane everyday problems such as getting the plumber to unblock the drain and what to have for dinner. Peaceful companionship in the evenings with a cup of tea developed a special significance.

The hospice outreach team of nurses and doctors became Steven's supporting lifeline helping him to manage his pain and the physical discomfort. He accepted advice from strangers sooner and more often than from me. The visiting nurse was fast becoming a confidant and friend. This pleased me, as Steven did not make friends easily.

I tried to do my best to manage the emotional and existential care—yet I needed support as well. Fortunately colleagues in the hospice were there to offer a shoulder to cry on when needed. Yet one day when the pharmacist questioned one of Steven's prescriptions I broke down, and told him I can do without this 'shit!' I have a dying husband at home. This was not like me, I am not generally rude to people. But I was tired after a day's work with dying patients. I felt helpless. How could I be treated just like any ordinary customer in a shop when I have so much grief to cope with, could he not see that? How could I be treated the same as anyone else? Standing alone, I was there with no one to help me. Losing my temper was a concern. Was this a sign of diminished emotional balance or was I just a grieving wife? Unfortunately I could not afford the luxury of grieving, because who would care for Steven if I was to give in to feelings of self-pity?

Steven was a good patient though, which helped me to remain focused and able to be there for him as well as do my nursing work. He managed his personal hygiene care, medicated himself and maintained his independence. This was a significant characteristic of his nature making his prognosis so much easier. He intended to stay home, away from hospital care, no matter how sick. As the independent proud man that he was, he wanted to be left to his own devices as much as possible. Steven welcomed old friends dropping in now that he had given up driving. Reminiscing about old times took his mind away from the body that had let him down now so badly.

Our boys decided to come home while their father was well enough to appreciate the visit. When Steven hears this, his anger flares up with a vengeance.

'I know you did this', he said, confronting me. 'You made them come home', he angrily accused me. 'I am not that sick.'

For some days afterwards he continued to be upset, but as the visit gets closer I sensed him calming down. The day the boys arrived was exciting. For the first time in months I felt secure as I embraced them at the airport. Their father greeted them with bear hugs, which was quite unlike him. He was appreciative of their visit. I noticed that they appeared to communicate better which seemed to me to be a significant change in their relationship. Like me, the boys seemed to get closer to their father now that he was a frail person, and not the strong difficult man of their childhood. The boys knew that this would probably be their last opportunity to see and to interact with him.

The end

It was now winter, so no more sitting in the sun. The garden Steven so loved was bare of leaves, the vegetables still in the ground and were left there. Steven could not cope with food very well these days and I also ate very little. It was the month of July and grey skies were the order of the day. It rained most of the time. It was when I turned sixty. Steven organised a party for this significant milestone in my life. He invited friends new and old to share the day. I suspected this may be his way of saying goodbye to everyone as well as wishing me a good life. We celebrated in style.

There was a lot to eat and to drink. It was sad that Steven failed to enjoy these pleasures at this time. I looked at him and noticed how he cut a sad figure, thin and bent. Not like the man I met so long ago. He used to be the life of the party, the last one to go home, but now pain rules his life.

A birthday party misses its mission without a cake. Steven helped me cut it after a speech. He talked about my restless inquisitive nature, my passion for running, and finished with the wish that I find myself one day and be happy.

He is very frail now, and I wondered how much more weight he could afford to lose. He never complained of pain but I could see he is suffering, and eventually agreed to take some extra pain relief. When I suggested I take holidays to be with him, in typically Steven fashion he asked, 'Do you think I am going to kick the bucket?' I found this significant because he never mentioned death and wondered if this was an introduction to a possible talk about his life ending, but it never happened. It hurts that this man who shared his life with me refused to share his death.

Three weeks after my birthday I made up my mind that it is time to stay home no matter what he said. Steven had reached a stage when he no longer could take the medication I put out for him each day. I found the tablets untouched. He needed supervision now with all of his activities. Each day brought further deterioration in his physical condition. After decided to stay at home with him, he stayed in bed and slept most of the day.

One day Steven was really sick. He did not take any food or fluids and the sound of his chest reminded me of my father's laboured lung towards the end of his life. The palliative care doctor who visited each day came and suggested a morphine infusion. My good nursing friend reminded me that should I need help she would be ready to come over anytime. I rang the boys to let them know that the end is not far off.

By two o'clock the next morning I was worried enough to ring my friend. I could not cope without some help, and she arrives twenty minutes later. After assessing Steven's condition she gave him more medication. As a nurse I knew I could have safely given him more but as his wife I was reluctant to do so. It is very difficult to be objective when it is your own husband. Then I phoned my son, who by now was back in London, to let him know that he would not make it home before his father dies. While still on the phone I look up as the door slowly opens, and my nursing friend whispers: 'He is gone, Susan', meaning that Steven had just died. I felt powerless as I tell my son that his father has just died. He breaks into sobs, I cannot even hug him, and have to do it again when ringing my other boy. Suddenly a feeling of utter loss and emptiness overcame me. The nurse helped me with washing Steven and putting him into clean pyjamas. Not seeing his unclad body until now shocked me when seeing how a robust man had become a virtual skeleton in only a few months. I notified the hospice doctor, called the funeral directors and opened the door to admit a number of my colleagues who, having heard of Steven's death, came to offer their condolences, and give me hugs and offers of help. There was coffee and toast for everyone as we waited for Steven to leave his home. No one left until he had left the house. Two nurses stripped the bed and washed the linen. I was thankful for colleagues who were also friends.

The family together

The boys came home for the funeral. We made the arrangements. We loved classical music so we chose some lovely pieces for the requiem Mass. There was a viewing of the body at the funeral parlour. This was my idea thinking that the boys would want to see their father for the last time. We went to the chapel together, but looking at the cold body was anything but pleasant. I hoped no one sensed my horror at seeing the body made up so un-Steven like. We remained only for a short time. That night over a hot Indian curry, red wine and old photos we even laughed as we remembered.

The funeral

Many friends and colleagues came to the funeral. I will never forget walking down the aisle with the coffin; the boys with some close friends were pallbearers. I was proud to have my sons with me as I walked ahead. One of the boys delivered a stirring eulogy and managed not to break down. I had lost my husband, but the feeling I had about his passing was gratitude for a good death and his relief from suffering.

When it is all over I felt lonely and sad. The boys returned overseas to their respective obligations, as did my sister who lives in Queensland to hers. There now only remained the countless flower arrangements and the cards letting me know the many thoughts and prayers people had for the family.

I realised that I had learnt a great deal about coping with the loss of the significant life partner during the months of Steven's illness. There is a vast difference between being with the sick person in the role of a professional carer and the intimate slow loss of a husband.

What has this taught me?

I thought I knew it all, caring for dying people and supporting the family. I thought I understood how grief touches them. But now that I had my private grief, I had to admit that real understanding comes from personally being there. Watching my husband slowly turn into a virtual skeleton, I did not only see a physical body becoming weaker but I also saw a strong independent mind trying to rule bodily disintegration. When you come face to face with similar situations as a nurse you accept it as part and parcel of the disease process, you support the family in their confusion at seeing their partner or father's slow death but you never know how they really suffer. As hard as the nurse tries to be empathic and understanding, it is never the same as knowing how it really is. Terminal illness as I saw it through the lens of Steven's cancer experience made us both more compatible, more loving and more understanding. The passage of the last six months of his life renewed our commitment to each other by demonstrating how life is indeed finite and therefore valuable. Forgotten were the plans that never came to fruition, the trips we never took or the expensive purchases we never made. We had each other, we knew each other and the small things mattered so much more.

What the nurse cannot fully understand about a patient's relationship with the family is the intimate thread that binds those people together, and how that manifests in a situation of bereavement. Each situation is unique and individual. I do not profess that the lesson my experience taught me is how every one manages death and dying in immediate families, but at least I was given an insight into deeper grief meanings that I could now confidently share and that I believed would makes me a better hospice nurse.

Face to face with death again

Returning to work I found that I had more humility and consideration for patients and the families in my care. I experienced more warmth toward the women who have lost their life's companions because I had some understanding for how they could be feeling. Now I could stand back and leave them space to grieve and invite them to ask for help. It was a liberating experience to realise how Steven's death enhanced my feeling of compassion and my nursing competency with dying patients and their families entrusted to my care. That was his legacy to the nursing speciality of palliative care. It is a pity that I could not tell him. This truly cemented my vocational path and strengthened my resolve to continue working in hospice even though I had reached retirement age. I stayed another fourteen years following Steven's death, and was convinced that I benefited from those years and am hopeful that the hospice gained as well.

4. Afterthought

Reflecting on my personal tragedies changing my life, I noted that the nursing culture I had been part of earlier had changed also. From saving lives I went to supporting dying people. I was truly transformed by the tragic realities that altered my approach to my profession, a truly transformative experience.

I offer all of this as the background to my practice not only as a general nurse but also as one who is competent in coping with the scene of death and dying personally.

Section Two

My Way of Getting There

In more than half a century of clinical nursing I never asked myself why I initially opted to work as a nurse. In the early 1950s nursing was the only health care profession willing to accept the educational qualifications of a new migrant. I had no other option because I wanted to be part of a caring profession. My expectations of nursing, however, were fulfilled. I enjoyed patient care and whatever the clinical world had to offer, and there was no need to ask why. Only recently have I been questioning the motivation behind these things, and now have began to explore the signposts that pointed to what could have signalled my future professional objectives.

When I wrote about the death of my father, I was examining my early leaning to helping in situations where people cannot care for themselves. It foreshadowed my becoming a nurse. The subsequent two stories spoke about the death of my mother and husband that indicated progression to palliative care and my comfort with remaining in that area of nursing.

My aim now is to look a little deeper and discover the cause of that mid career change.

This section outlines the building blocks of the study by examining four areas:
- Writing that marries personal experience with transformation—the methodology of auto-ethnography;
- Partnership of narrative and knowledge;
- Power of knowledge—patterns of knowing;
- Consciousness: the patient and the nurse's knowledge building.

I conclude with a discussion of the birth of the hospice and palliative care movement and the personalities who were responsible for it.

5. Writing that marries personal experience with transformation:

Auto-ethnography

> *Joyful moments come with the presence of others with faces turned to other faces, with connections that allow isolated individuals refuge in the welcoming of another's hand.*[1]

Like Ron Pelias I also reached out for a 'telling essence' because I wanted connections to the best methodology for my research that would explore my progress to palliative care and my presence in the years of helping people in pain and suffering. I wanted to tell a story that would stir emotional feelings in those who hear or read it. I felt it had to be a narrative approach

When I understood auto-ethnography, it took my breath away as it adopted the role for me of a 'helping partner'. This was when I began appreciating the value of what Pelias calls 'genuine connection'.[2] Suddenly it was clear to me that auto-ethnography was the ideal way to do this research because, as well as giving permission to use personal experience/musings/thoughts/opinions as data, it also 'invites others to become involved with a life, engage with [its] contingencies, finitude, embededness in shared being'.[3]

But what is auto-ethnography?

I first encountered the term auto-ethnography through reading Ellis and Bochner's work.[4] Their chapter in the second edition of Denzin and Lincoln's *Handbook of Qualitative Research* is a seminal academic reference spearheading auto-ethnographic research. As a

---

1. RJ Pelias 'On The Joy Of Connections', in *Qualitative Communication Research*, 1/2 (2012): 163–167.
2. Pelias "on The Joy Of Connections", 163.
3. AP Bochner, 'Suffering Happiness', in *Qualitative Communication Research*, 1/2 (2012): 225.
4. C Ellis and AP Bochner, 'Autoethnography, Personal Narrative, Reflexivity', in *Handbook of Qualitative Research*, second edition, edited by NK Denzin and YS Lincoln (Thousand Oaks, California: Sage Publications, 2000).

clinician investigating the culture of palliative care from the 'inside', I discovered through their work that I could understand myself not only as the researcher but also as the one researched. This was very helpful for me.

In auto-ethnography I write the research (graphy) about myself (auto) in relation to culture (ethno). This privileges 'a deep understanding of self, culture and the interaction between the two'.[5]

Bochner and Ellis write of it as an evocative study of self-awareness within a culture, a research method that uses personal experience, and focuses on the lived experience by keeping conversation going that clears the way to shared understanding of living.[6]

This theory gave support to my view of life and nursing as a professional involvement, because auto-ethnographic research and writing not only explores my experience of a practice but also describes the culture I connect, work and live with.[7] Defining this methodology, while useful, is not necessary, because as Chang says 'auto-ethnography means different things to different people' and it is not easy to restrict it to a single concept.[8] Each researcher owns an individual social awareness and welcomes the freedom to use a personal introspective writing style. Auto-ethnographic texts emerge from the researcher's bodily stand-point as she or he continually recognises and interprets the residual traces that culture inscribes upon her/him from interaction with others. This corporeal textual orientation rejects the notion that 'lived experience can only be represented indirectly through quotations from field notes, observations and interviews'.[9] In the auto-ethnographic research style the investigator is the epistemological and ontological nexus upon which the research process turns. Auto-ethnographers, especially

---

5. 'From "Bitch" To "Mentor": A Doctoral Student's Story Of Self-Change And Mentoring', in *The Qualitative Report*, 17, article 59 (2012): 4, viewed 10 July 2013, http://www.nova.edu/ssss/QR/QR17/gearity.pdf
6. AP Bochner 'Suffering Happiness', in *Qualitative Communication Research*, 1/2 (2012): 209–229; C Ellis *'The Ethnographic I'* (Walnut Creek, Lanham, New York, Oxford: Alta Mira Press, 2004).
7. Ellis *'The Ethnographic I'*, 37.
8. H Chnag, *Autoethnography As method* (Walnut Creek CA: Left Coast Press, 2008), 46.
9. NK Denzin 'The Many Faces Of Emotionality: Reading Persona', in *Investigating Subjectivity*, edited by C Ellis & MG Flaherty (Newbury Park, London: Sage Publications, 1992), 20 .

those using an evocative style, argue that a self-reflexive critique of ones position as a researcher inspires readers to reflect critically upon their own life experience, their construction of self and their interaction with others within socio-historical contexts.

Auto-ethnography in this project is the medium that has enabled me to explain my reasons for nursing patients who will die. It has enabled me to share my feelings about what drives me. This methodology allows you to be aware of a novel way of unpacking uncertainties and doubts that as a researcher you continually meet in what you are doing.

While searching for a guiding theory and methodology I first gravitated towards an ethnographic approach. I soon realised however that being outside a culture was not helpful. As an insider I achieved better understanding because it is more comforting to '. . . dialogically connect the ethical, respectful self to nature and [the] worldly environment'.[10]

In the literature I discovered that anthropology and the social sciences question the role of the researcher in ethnographic studies, and ask why ethnographers need to stand outside the culture they are investigating. Crawford has argued that 'taking the ethnographic turn, living and writing the ethnographic life, is essentially a self-report of personal experience' and as such 'the ethnographer is unavoidably in the ethnography one way or another, however subtly or obviously'.[11] While searching for data researchers inevitably become part of the culture they are involved in researching. Just by putting a foot inside another's domain one becomes a member of that culture even if only tentatively and in some limited way. Shaffir supports this when he writes that there is a degree of self-presentation in ethno methodology and acknowledges that he was often drawn to the practices and beliefs of the community he was researching at the time.[12]

Anthropological ethnographer Ruth Behar sees a blurring of ethnographic research genres and talks of the 'creative non-fiction [and] fluid field of hybrid texts [or] stories based on the testimony

---

10. NK Denzin 'Interpretive ethnography, 28/5 (1999): 510.
11. L Crawford, 'Personal Ethnography', in *Communication Monographs,* 63 (1996): 158.
12. W Shaffir, 'Doing Ethnography: Reflections On Finding Your Way', in *Journal of Contemporary Ethnography,* 28/6 (1999): 676–686.

of lived experience.'[13] A study in nursing ethnography of reflexive fieldwork demonstrates how embodied use of the senses 'led into areas that otherwise would have remained unexplored.'[14] The nurse does not only rely on readouts from instruments to diagnose a problem with the patient she cares for, but uses all physical senses to supplement findings.

Amanda Coffey in *The Ethnographic Self*, foreshadows as inevitable that the personal will combine with the 'cultural' in future ethnographic research activities because 'we are a part of what we study and [are] affected by cultural contexts shaped by our fieldwork.'[15] Deborah Reed-Danahay supports auto-ethnographic research,[16] but Rosanna Hertz foreshadows ethical issues with the personal presence in auto-ethnography when the writer's personality is displayed.[17] On the other hand Mykhalovskiy is convinced that his personal story is engaging and readable.[18] Charmaz & Mitchell challenge the concept of a 'silent authorship' and maintain that openly using the author's presence and voice gives the research substance and style. 'Evocative forms of writing are not merely desirable; they are essential.'[19] I have welcomed this standpoint as it has opened the door to my being honest and unrestricted while allowing me to look at 'involving readers' imaginative participation'[20] when describing personal experience.

Carolyn Ellis's reaction to Leon Anderson is helpful as she has maintained that auto-ethnography should be more analytical than evocative in being a research methodology.[21] Reading this coincided with Ellis watching on her television the graphic horror of levees

---

13. R Behar, *The Vulnerable Observer* (Boston: Beacon Press, 1996), 476 .
14. D Edvardson and A Street, 'Sense or No-Sense: The Nurse As Embodied Ethnographer', in *International Journal of Nursing Practice*, 13 (2007): 24.
15. A Coffey, *The Ethnographic Self* (London: Sage Publications, 1999), 37.
16. D Reed-Danahay, *Auto-Ethnography* (Oxford/New York: Berg Publishers, 1997).
17. R Hertz, *Reflexivity and Voice* (Thousand Oaks, CA: Sage Publications, 1997)
18. E Mykhalovskiy, 'Reconsidering "Table Talk": Critical Thoughts On The Relationship Between Sociology, Autobiography And Self-Indulgence', in *Reflexivity and Voice*, edited by R Hertz, Sage Publications, Thousand Oaks, CA: Sage Publications, 1997).
19. K Charmaz, and RG Mitchell Jnr 'The Myth Of Silent Authorship: Self, Substance, And Style In Ethnographic Writing', in *Reflexivity and Voice*, edited by R Hertz, Sage Publications, Thousand Oaks, CA: Sage Publications, 1997), 195.
20. K Charmaz, and RG Mitchell Jnr 'The Myth Of Silent Authorship', 195.
21. C Ellis *Revision: Autoethnographic Reflections On Life And Work*, (Walnut Creek, CA: Left Coast Press Inc, 2009).

breaking up in hurricane-ravaged New Orleans. She was about to start writing a commentary on Anderson's views but could not go on as seeing people drown while doing this stopped her from writing. Ellis's distress at the massive horror momentarily halted her line of thought, only to return later with her pain and discomfort around auto-ethnography being perceived by Anderson as seriously scientific. She has maintained that auto-ethnography is meant to be evocative, and is the best way to paint a word picture of emotional involvement in human experience that readers will identify with in their own lives. Ellis wants to stay with 'the world of experience, feel it, taste it, sense it, live in it'.[22] She uses her heart not only her head in her auto-ethnographic work. I prefer being evocative also, because I can only be truly reflective when I use my 'positive' emotional self in response to the pain and suffering of my patients.[23] To enter the world of another is the response to an invitation to become involved on a similar plane. The 'inviter' then becomes intrigued and engrossed by the shared involvement. The story shared needs to be clear, easily understood and explicit. In auto-ethnography I am the storyteller and to an extent, the story. You come into my world and should feel my very existence, pain and joy.

Auto-ethnographic Researcher

> *Auto-ethnography is setting a scene, telling a story, weaving intricate connection among life and art, experience and theory and evocation and explanation . . . and then letting go hoping for readers who will bring the same careful attention to your words in the context of their own lives.*[24]

I direct my stories, like Holman-Jones, towards the readers' careful attention, because the benefit of auto-ethnographic research and

---

22. C Ellis, *Revision*, 431.
23. C Johns , *Being Mindful, Easing Suffering, Reflections On Palliative Care* (London and New York: Jessica Kingsley Publishers, 2004), 84
24. S Holman-Jones, 'Autoethnography: Making The Personal Political' in *Handbook of Qualitative Research,* third edition edited by NK Denzin and YS Lincoln (Thousand Oaks, CA: Sage Publications, 2005), 763.

writing is in the ability to create engagement with the reader who hopefully will reflect on their own life in the context of mine.

The introspective and narrative character of auto-ethnography informs the fundamental nature of my study. As a methodology it encourages me to be in the present and in the past, almost simultaneously. In practical terms this means that I examine and interpret phenomena and feelings at any given time. At each step I consider what happened before and its relevance to the present with implications for the future. As such, I realise that auto-ethnography is a conversation with myself and a dialogue with the reader.[25] As the researcher I am directed to a place where the story describes life perceptions and interpretations of my world. In practical terms it means that I examine my lived experience and refuse to be only objective or purposeful. It means that what I want to achieve is an understanding of myself as a person and how I am affected by the culture of which I am a member.

My personal story is written and will remain the autobiographical hub to which I return from time to time. The story of my father's death deeply affected me as a young woman and it lay dormant until my study of auto-ethnography brought it to life, and as such I am aware of how 'self interviewing' is the initial step in my data collection. I depend on my lived experience as I relate to the world that houses it.[26] I engage in ongoing reflectivity because it 'harnesses my energies',[27] and that is how I identify the conscious acts that commute between my life worlds. The concept of consciousness that Ellis mentions is acknowledged in the multiplicity of my human involvement. My body houses a wealth of individual personal models from its lifespan; I am the product of a collage of experience. I am a parent, someone's child, someone's spouse, a nurse, a researcher, a friend or just an interested observer, all at the same time. These complex personalities interact and could emerge as one entity in the reality of living. I can safely say that a long life offered me multiple opportunities to be a

---

25. HG Gadamer, *Truth and Method*.
26. M Van Manen, 'From Meaning To Method', *Qualitative Health Research*, 7/3 (1999) 345–369.
27. C Johns, *Engaging Reflection In Practice* (Oxford: Blackwell Publishing, Oxford, 2006), 6.

conglomerate of beings, and I am comfortable with auto-ethnography as the best way to relay that research message.

Auto-ethnography, however, is a complex concept. Each researcher uses an individually special way to offer a social presence within an auto-ethnographic picture. Alford's narrative tells of her hospital admission when undignified treatment made her feel like 'only a piece of meat'.[28] Waymer analyses a black man's confrontation with white privilege in a performance text of the personal distress of racism.[29] Lisa Tillman uses poetry to describe a community of gay men processing their response to the United States Presidential elections in 2004,[30] and Perry in a dialogue shares the pain of her father's death with her academic mentor.[31] On reading these I recognise the possibility of a free hand in writing my experiential narrative.

The driving force behind this study is my interest in the question of what attracted me to the care of people who did not recover their health, those who eventually died. Pelias is convincing when he says the methodology of auto-ethnography 'let's you use yourself to get to the culture, a culture that for [you] is familiar and [you feel] an essential part of it'.[32] I firmly believe this, by researching through the auto-ethnographic lens I am reminded that as a member of palliative care nursing for twenty or more years I can speak with some authority about caring for terminally ill people. I know the belief system, personal values, spirituality and nurturing. This study deals with a unique way of telling a 'one of a kind story' that eventually brings the culture and my experience together with self-reflectivity and the voice of others in palliative care nursing.[33] As the auto-ethnographer

---

28. EF Alford, 'Only A Piece Of Meat: One Patient's Reflection On Her Eight-Day Hospital Visit', in *Qualitative Inquiry*, 12/3 (2006) 596.
29. D Waymer, D 2008, 'A Man: An Autoethnographic Analysis Of Black Male Identity Negotiation', in *Qualitative Inquiry*, 14/6 (2008): 968–989.
30. LM Tillman, 'The State Of Unions; Activism (And In-Activism) In Decision 2004', Conference presentation, University of Chicago, Urbana Campus, 2005.
31. J Perry, 'Dialogical Intersection: The Death Of A Father', in *Journal of Loss and Trauma* (2001): 161–182.
32. Pelias, 2003, p. 372.
33. C Smith, 'Epistemological Intimacy: A Move To Autoethnography', in *International Journal of Qualitative Methods*, 4/2 (2005): 1-7.

I stand naked before the reader. There is an unashamed honesty in sharing myself openly.

However, when I chose auto-ethnography I discovered that nursing science rarely explores the nurse's individual personality, let alone researches it. From experience I consistently saw the nurse as a team worker. Nurses rarely talk of themselves in the first person 'I' and do not prescribe to individual practice or theoretical interaction. Nursing is a culture of 'us' and 'our' world. It is difficult to locate literature that speaks of the nurse as an individual.

In Australia there were attempts made by a small number of nurse researchers to give voice to the nurse as a specific person within a group. Megan-Jane Johnston discussed the concept of '*Reflective topical autobiography*' concerning nurse education.[34] She even suggested that a reflective autobiographical approach could be a useful research method and even become a 'prerequisite to undertaking research in nursing'.[35] But she left it at that. Bruni[36] and White[37] questioned how researching the 'personal' would be acceptable in the climate of a strongly evidence based health care system. The area of mental health care was the first group to break down this barrier with an auto-ethnographic narrative inquiry into 'The Experiences Of Being An Adult Child Of A Parent With Psychosis'.[38] Globally auto-ethnographic nursing research came out of Northern Ireland[39] the United Kingdom and the United States of America.[40] Authors in these countries also dealt with nurse education. My study however is taking

---

34. MJ Johnstone, 'Reflective Topical Autobiography: An Under Utilized Interpretive Research In Nursing', in *Collegian*, 6/1 (1999): 24–29.
35. Johnstone, 'Reflective Topical Autobiography', 29.
36. N Bruni, 'Crisis Of Visibility: Ethical Dilemmas Of Autoethnographic Research', in *Qualitative Research Journal*, 2/1, (2002): 24–32.
37. S White, 'Autoethnography—An Appropriate Methodology', in *Qualitative Research Journal*, 3/2 (2003): 22-32.
38. K Foster, M McAllister and L O'Brien, 2006, 'Extending The Boundaries: Autoethnography As An Emergent Method In Mental Health Nursing Research', in *International Journal of Mental Health Nursing*, 15 (2006): 44–53.
39. J Wright, J 2008, 'Searching One's Self: The Autoethnography Of A Nurse Teacher', in *Journal Of Research In Nursing*, 13/4 (2008): 338–347.
40. P Burnard, P 2007, 'Seeing The Psychiatrist: An Autoethnographic Account', in *Journal Of Research In Nursing*, 14 (2007): 808–814; T Muncey, T 2005, 'Doing Autoethnography', in *International Journal of Qualitative Methods*', 4/1 (2005): .

a different approach as it goes beyond the nurse as a team worker to find the individual personality that desires to change her practice.

As the auto-ethnographer I am a human being with a variety of experiences and emotions, all of which will always come through in my writing. Auto-ethnographic writing does not only tell 'stories about [myself] garnished with detail',[41] but also includes interactive dialogue with others about their experience. Good writing needs to contain a whole range of emotions, even when addressing the subject of ordinary everyday life. In writing about happiness, for instance, there needs to be a bit of sadness in order to make the happiness meaningful.[42] Researching my topic is like a journey that begins by focusing on the goal or the place of arrival. As in training for and then running marathons, the end is in the distance, and along the way many things evolve. The runner, while knowing the dangers, tends to ignore much of the negatives. The road is rocky, there is pain, there are detours, but eventually there is the triumph in the arrival. The same can be the case in nursing in palliative care settings.

Jessica and I

> On my return to the hospice I found Jessica's bed empty. She died last night. While I knew her death was inevitable, the pain at her loss was real. Jessica was a friend as well as a patient. Only yesterday she was here warm, her heart hardly beating, today I feel the need to remember.
>
> Jessica and I go back a long way in terms of nurse/patient relationships. Our path first crossed two years previously when she was admitted for treatment of an infected foot. As a paraplegic she easily traumatised her lower limbs. Jessica was confined to a wheelchair for twenty years. Paralysis was the result of aggressive radiotherapy that destroyed her spinal nerves; she was only 30 years old at the time. Her recovery amazed all who knew her and they watched as Jessica set out to live life her way quickly establishing her independence.
>
> During a childless marriage she frequently felt Brian her husband's scorn for her lack of academic achievement. Confined

---

41. Chang, *Autoethnography As Method,* 149.
42. AP Bochner, 'Suffering Happiness', 226.

to a wheelchair she managed to gain an arts degree and completed two years of legal studies. Due to her deteriorating health and Brian's work commitments she never achieved her goal of having double degrees. An interstate move cut her off from her friends and family but she quickly adjusted to her new environment, made new friends easily. Her interest in others endeared her to all she met. Neighbours, Brian's work colleagues, medical personnel, the local shopkeepers, the hairdresser, garbage collector and her gardener all became her friends. Nursing her presented a unique cultural environment of sharing personal histories. I found her life a fascinating collection of 'bad luck' for anyone else, but for Jessica each was a new challenge. Her moral strength was called upon soon after moving to this town. The radiation therapy mentioned earlier that paralysed her legs affected bladder functions as well with accompanying incontinence and pain. To relieve this a delicate procedure was performed, one that necessitated the wearing of a stoma bag. She managed this appliance well coming to the out patient department for visits occasionally. My second encounter with her was during such a visit as she drove herself to the hospital in her beloved Mercedes. She departed that day with a cheery smile and I did not see her for another year or so. Her visit always left me light hearted and thankful for being in a profession that allowed witnessing such personal triumphs. Jessica's next trial came in the guise of a bowel obstruction, another result of the past radiation treatment. This problem could eventually only be effectively managed with the formation of another stoma. During that operation she was found to have a new cancerous growth. The decision was against treatment until she recovered from the surgery. This never happened because Jessica never recovered enough to have cancer treatment.

The postoperative period was difficult; her pain was unrelenting and difficult to control. That is when she was transferred to the care of pain management specialists in the hospice unit. And that is when our relationship grew stronger. I was appointed as her primary nurse—the one who looked after her whenever I was on duty. Jessica was genuinely pleased. I believe she saw me as a friend and trusted me. In the nursing culture having continuity of care that primary nursing enables, is a precious commodity. It promotes effective nurse patient connectedness. Even like this we went through difficult times. Pain continued to be a problem as was the generalised infection *whose cause was never found. Both Jessica and her husband set their mind on a curing model of care and many invasive procedures were initiated.*

Her treatment included intravenous antibiotic administration and active resuscitation should that be required (which was not the norm in the hospice). Hospice staff questioned both these aspects of her care. We rarely use this process to keep a patient alive. However I accepted that Jessica's case was different. She had to be supported in her battle even if only to give her comfort amid the haze of painful hours. Her medical team spent time consulting and communicating with both Jessica and her husband. The doctors also went on hoping that she would manage to go home. Unfortunately she lost much of the joy she always exhibited when feeling better, she barely took any nourishment. During this time Jessica looked forward to being alone with me. This was when she spoke of her fears of dying, how much she still wanted to accomplish and her relationship with her husband. She told me of personal matters that she maintained she never shared with anyone before. We connected on an even plane. Jessica was in need of confiding her feelings and I was a trusted listener.

Most of our communications took place during intimate comfort care. Changing two stoma bags was an art during which we spoke of life. Looking back I realised how during precious practical caring times the nurse achieves more than just the physical care. That is when two human beings can come together and build up trust in each other. As it was, Jessica and I just kept hoping for a miracle and for a time it looked as if we were winning. Jessica again improved, she 'picked up' so much so that the physiotherapist encouraged her to use weights to strengthen the arms, essential in facilitating transfer manoeuvres of the paraplegic. From then on we had fun in the shower where she loved to get soaked and sometimes soaked me. I found great delight in generously using her Chanel No5 soap and powder and let her luxuriate in the pleasure of having her face indulged with liberal application of a particularly expensive Clarins product. During the hour and a half it took me to make Jessica comfortable we listened to each other's life stories.

Jessica's pride and joy was Muffy a Siamese cat that frequently turned up to sit on her bed and purr away her pleasure at being with her mistress. The cat replaced the child she never had. Jessica loved animals. Jock a little white dog I often share with a friend visited her [just missing Muffy] and he became a firm favourite also.

Then one day Jessica had a relapse and her physical condition rapidly deteriorated. The intravenous line was reinserted, antibiotics were given again and we all kept hoping. That was the end of the fun in the shower, her face became thinner and she spoke less. Yet there was always a smile when she saw me. The following experience I will never forget.

I suffer from cold hands summer and winter. Jessica playfully shivered whenever I touched her and told me with a grin to keep away. Three days before she died she took my cold hands and put them under her sheets in an effort to warm them, a testament of the love and trust she had for me. As her strength ebbed we did not speak much, touching replaced words I respected all the little personal requests of the past: to make the room warm, open the curtains, special pillows at the foot of the bed, using that face cream, and yes the Chanel No5. This also helped me as just by being with her I faced the end of a relationship a little easier.

I believe Jessica and I became firm friends during a difficult time. As the nurse I recognised who I was; a skilled and competent professional. As a woman and human being I was aware of my personal understanding of Jessica in all her moods and went along with what ever she wanted. It is often easier to have a deaf ear when something is too hard to do. But by being sensitive to and wearing the 'other's' shoes it is easy to comply with the smallest wish.

Jessica gave me support to believe in myself and I in turn accepted all of her care as a privilege.

Parting thoughts

In summary, my choice for auto-ethnography was prompted by an attraction to a method that investigates the 'lived' experience in a style of ethnography that delegates the researcher to be the subject and object of the study. Auto-ethnography employs narrative story telling that encourages reflexivity with the 'audience' whose response generates data. The evocative auto-ethnographic researcher, by first exploring personal experience, creates a space where relationships are analysed and refocused when connecting with those outside the space. It is a methodology that first and foremost relies on researching and writing the self, yet there is no limit put on the way one uses that concept. I did not only rely on myself to tell the research story but gathered others to share their experience of palliative care. With the interviewees I shared moments that were for me auto-ethnographic. As the observer and the observed I was completely comfortable with being the researcher and the research. I looked inward and outward when I identified the ethnographic other. Getting fully into the other's head, heart and body and acting back on the prevailing culture is when interaction between the other and I became a reality. That is what will tell the story of what I consider to be the nursing vocation, natural caring abilities and the resulting transformation.

6. Partnership of narrative and knowledge

Doreen's story

I introduce this section once again with a story. The following brief narrative describes patient/nurse connectedness. It depicts Doreen and myself as central characters of the story by changing the writing into verbal action where the body and the voice could not be separated from the mind.[43] The narrative of my day in the hospice has much of the building blocks of my introspective story telling style. It describes the deep patient/nurse connectedness and my understanding the consequences of my actions. I agree with Chase that narrative makes the self the central character either as actor or as an interested observer in an activity.[44]

> *Doreen is in pain and discomfort. I am about to give her a wash and dress her wound that is becoming more of a problem. Doreen is an uncomplaining woman who suffers from advanced cancer of the cervix, one of the most discomforting of women's diseases. I give a pain relieving medication before disturbing her. Unfortunately she had some not long so long ago and obviously needs a larger dose before I can begin. She tells me the pain is really bad. I decide to wait until the doctor comes and can possibly order more medication. When I notice him sitting by her bed I quickly go up to listen and learn of any possible treatment changes. Doreen true to her uncomplaining nature denies any bad pain when asked. As the doctor stands up to walk away I stop him and tell him of Doreen's increased*

---

43. Chase, 'Response to "The Concept Of Nursing Presence"'; Holman-Jones, 'Autoethnography: Making The Personal Political'.
44. Chase, 'Response to "The Concept Of Nursing Presence"'.

> *discomfort and how she almost begged me for help this morning. After cross-examining Doreen the doctor eventually orders an increase to her morphine that I give immediately. The result was amazing. Doreen relaxed in a little while and I could do her morning care of wash, wound care etc. and she was comfortable during the process.*
>
> *'I feel so good. I am sorry you have days off now and won't see you until Friday' is her comment when I go by her room to wish her well at the end of the shift. That was the last time I saw Doreen.*
>
> *A note in my journal two days later:*
>
> *I just read in the newspaper obituaries that Doreen died yesterday. I am sorry I did not see her again but the last time when I cared for her I made her happy and comfortable. The wounds were dressed appropriately; I fought for and got orders for the added pain relief so she would have had a comfortable death.*

This sounds as if I brushed aside the loss of a patient by saying that I did all I could under the circumstances, but that was far from my mind. I could not help but keep wondering if she had been given enough pain relief before she died, was she comfortable, was her family with her? I knew that to continue thinking about a patient after her death is not healthy, but Doreen stayed with me for sometime. I was working the day of her funeral; being there may have provided the appropriate closure for the relationship. As it turned out I was left with asking myself what could justify my feelings for this patient? Then it dawned on me that Doreen trusted me in a special way. I proved to her that I not only promise but also deliver. I was proud of my strength the day when I stood up to the doctor in the face of his opposition to increase her pain relief. Doreen was rather particular with her thanks. It was not a simple 'thank you' but a deeply felt gratitude that created a warm feeling in me.

By starting this section with a story I wish introduce the auto-ethnographic narrative style of writing and indicate my intention to go on in this manner. Narratives are found in multiple forms. They may be constructed field notes, evocative personal stories, multi-layered accounts of experience, introspective confessionals and co-

constructed created accounts.[45] Doreen's story by being evocative indicated my intense involvement with her. Yet reading the postscript written after her death all I wanted to do was apologise for my terseness. That is when I realised that there were two narrative models in the brief layered account—one the emotional feeling person, the other a nurse providing information about her patient.

The auto-ethnography that directs my research is evocative narrative inquiry. I write that way to reach the innermost beings of my readers. What I mean is that I want to appeal to people's existential understanding of my suffering and their readiness to replicate the experience. I want my story to be felt by others as it felt for me.

Being the clinician, narrative writing did not come easy and made scholarship a difficult aim; at least that is what I thought. I wondered what 'scholarship' actually was, and was it essential in a personal historical account of experience?

This question hung over me, and threateningly so for sometime. When I asked one of my professors how he would define scholarship, instead of telling me he directed me to the library to view a book that left me cold. The word scholarship has scared me ever since. To me it indicated long complex phrases that needed explaining in the first place. Yet eventually I came to a gradual understanding that scholarship may be the community of people whose work I read, who became my friends by teaching me through their writing. It is also the people I have met at conferences, but the most important learning and scholarship came from patients I nursed, their tolerance of suffering, their trust and their openness were the scholarly theses that taught me much. In those situations I never used complex verbal communication. Understanding happened by appealing to the essential humanness of those I cared for with awareness of my own emotions while being truly present. My kind of scholarship is the power behind my learning that shares the learnt experience.

---

45. C Ellis, 'Creating Criteria: An Ethnographic Short Story', in *Qualitative Inquiry*, 6/2 (2000): 273–277; JL Kincheloe and P McLaren, 2000, 'Rethinking Critical Theory And Qualitative Research, in *Handbook of Qualitative Research*, second edition, edited by NK Denzin and YS Lincoln, (Thousand Oaks, CA: Sage Publications); NZ Denzin, and YS Lincoln, editors 2000, *Handbook of Qualitative Research*, second edition (Thousand Oaks, CA: Sage Publications, 2000).

Remember where you are

Having explored the way I am likely to write the study I better explain why I believe that story telling and scholarship are important. Auto-ethnographic methodology prescribes awareness of the self within a culture and indicates that personal experiential writing is at the heart of the research.

The stories in this part are the backdrop of my professional development and urge me to focus on discovering the reasons for my change from a healing model of care to concentrating on end of life issues. To make all this clear I will focus on where, when and why this change or transformation happened. Was it an epiphany or could it have been a change of caring values that experience often brings about.[46] In my case I assume that personal grief is the catalyst that alerted me to my changed caring attitudes. I developed awareness of nursing's wide horizon of caring and knowledge base, and found that patient care is not built on health promotion only, but also on the moral attitude of the nurse who relates to personal beliefs.[47] Revisiting the three family bereavements I noticed a progressive change in life ideals that concurred with first the helplessness in the face of the agony of my father's painful end, proceeding to my mother's death and culminating in acceptance of the demise of my life's partner.

Narrative and story telling is at the heart of auto-ethnographic research and writing that invites this method of introducing the thesis with personal stories. Now it is time to deal with knowledge making and some philosophical matters. In the name of narrative and scholarship I now appeal to knowledge that is gained from experience and ask for the extent of knowledge gathering in nursing. The concept of knowledge is many sided; every one who practices

---

46. J Mezirow, J 1994, 'Understanding Transformation Theory', in *Adult Education Quarterly,* 44/4 (1994): 222-232.
47. C Gastmans, 'Care As A Moral Attitude', in *Nursing Ethics,* 6/3 (1999): 214-223; JB Hopkinson, CE Hallettt, and A Luker, KA 2003, 'Caring for dying people in hospitals', in *Journal of Advanced Nursing,* vol. 44/5 (2003): 525-; Y Wengstrom, and M Ekedahl, M 2006, 'The Art Of Professional Development And Caring In Cancer Nursing', in *Nursing and Health Sciences,* 8 (2006): 20-26.

a trade, a profession or a vocation has a different fountain where knowledge comes from. One eventually gets a qualification that satisfies that thirst. Nursing however is one of those professions where curiosity is never fully satisfied. The nurse comes face to face with new knowledge as long as she is in practice. Every situation with another patient offers a new challenging experience that invariably foreshadows the next event or problem.[48] It is never ending and that is why a nurse is ready to learn anew every day.

But what is nursing knowledge? Is involvement with people's physical and emotional selves so special that it needs a large knowledge base with a range of options? Well yes, nursing knowledge is so special that for the purpose of this study I use only a certain specific segment of it, because theory of transformation and interpretive hermeneutic philosophy of nursing is my focus.[49] This work does not deal with physical symptom management. The focus addresses the nurse personally.

7. Power of knowledge—patterns of knowing

The basic structure of my understanding of care transformation involves patterns of knowing. Carper as early as 1978 identified four patterns that Meleis later used in her discussion of knowing in nursing.[50] The patterns deal with nursing science, personal knowledge concerned with relationships, art of nursing and ethics. Maturing in my professional outlook and ongoing personal life experience makes it easier to ask questions. The knowledge base I come from is observational skills, clinical findings and a great deal of sense data that keeps me open to a more universal point of view.[51] Epistemic view of knowledge making is partly what forms my understanding of

---

48. Gadamer, *Truth and Method*, 335–357.
49. M Newman, *Health As Expanding Consciousness*, second edition, (Sudbury: Jones and Bartlet Publishers, 1994); MA Newman, *Transforming Presence* (Philadelphia: FA Davis Company, 2008); RR Parse, 1981, *Man-Living-Health: A Theory of Nursing* (New York, Chichester, Brisbane, Toronto John Wiley and Sons Publishers, 1981); AI Meleis, *Theoretical Nursing*; ME Rogers, ME 1970, *The Theoretical Basis Of Nursing* (Philadelphia: FA Davis Company, 1970).
50. AI Meleis, editor, *Theoretical Nursing*, fourth edition (Philadelphia Lippincot, Williams and Wilkins Publishers, 2007).
51. Gadamer, *Truth and Method*, 17.

the how and why of my progress to palliative caring. Meleis writes of three views of knowing and they are ones that I adopt to underpin my understanding of nursing transformation.[52]

The received view

The received view usually indicates '… a set of ideas that are not to be challenged—the philosophical equivalent of being carved in stone'.[53]

At the beginning, as I entered the nursing profession, this view directed my practice. I accepted what I believed was the 'truth' as I did not know any other. I was comfortable with it at the time as I began my knowledge gathering. Empirical knowing was directed by procedural scientific norms that dictated praxis. Reflecting on bedside nursing work I recall that the trend of not questioning authority was a part of most of my early clinical practice. No matter how at times I doubted its wisdom I was advised to follow the accepted line. Experience of 'do as you are told' followed me even as recently as the present century when in 2004 I was told in no uncertain terms by a much younger less experienced nurse never to discard empty drug boxes. The reason was never explained to me but it was a typical local rule that was followed along lines of 'received view'. Someone some time in the past decided on a 'local' by-law and not many questioned it. I felt bullied and humiliated.

Perceived view

My progress to the next phase that Meleis calls 'perceived viewing'[54] was gained by experiencing the world of nursing through praxis learning: remembering and understanding. There I met varied knowledge patterns in the form of new challenges. The more deeply I delved into the culture of nursing work the more I realised that it is not only learning scientific procedures, but balancing that with theory that justified and complemented praxis. This was most noticeable when I became aware of nursing as a caring focus on '… the human health experience' by more inclusive consciousness of the patient

---

52. Meleis, *Theoretical Nursing*, 488–89.
53. Meleis, *Theoretical Nursing*, 489.
54. Meleis, *Theoretical Nursing*, 491.

as a well-rounded human being, not only a sick physical body.[55] Knowledge gathering at this stage happened through the experience of being 'there'. I built a solid base for my professional involvement by participation in the illness experience of the patient.[56] I soon realised that my praxis action was often not based on a scientific presage but on an intuitive response to the situation I was in. According to Polanyi this is knowing without actual scientific reasoning.[57] The intuitive response is the result of experience in clinical situations.[58] I frequently found that the perceived view of my skill development was difficult to describe in the light of empiric values only. I felt that I often proceeded on a path of aesthetic patterning that embodied and enriched my understanding of 'nursing experience that is not accessible through other ways of knowing'.[59] I often reflected at the end of a working day on how patients shared their problems and fears while having a bed bath. On the day he died, the last words of Joel reminded me of this. He said: 'you did something right, I feel better'. With that he went to sleep and remained peaceful until he died.

I thought about this and came to the conclusion that the 'right' thing I did was simply be there for him. I listened, used gentle touch and did not hurry. There was silence in the room and I just responded as his demeanour dictated. I read his body / mind messages correctly. This perceptive way of understanding underwrote the reason for my involvement with illness, healing, death and dying. Working with it was easy but when it came to verbalizing it I was lost for words in the language of medical science or evidence based theory. Outcomes arising from nurse/patient connectedness are mainly existential, and are much better relayed through narratives, poetry or reflective journals. A story is far the best medium to explore, for argument's sake, suffering, compassion or mourning.[60]

---

55. MA Newman, *Transforming Presence* (Philadelphia: FA Davis, 2008), 16.
56. C Johns, *Engaging Reflection In Practice* (Oxford: Blackwell Publishing, 2006).
57. M Polanyi, *The Tacit Dimension* (New York: Garden City, 1966).
58. Meleis, *Theoretical Nursing*, 70.
59. JM Sorrell, 'Remembrance Of Things Past Through Writing: Aesthetic Patterns Of Knowing In Nursing', in *Advances in Nursing Science*, vol. 17/1 (1994): 60–70.
60. ME O'Brien, *The Nurse's Calling*, (New York/Mahwah, NJ: Paulist Press, 2001); Sorrell, 'Remembrance Of Things Past'.

That is why practical hands-on involvement develops sensitivity to existential concerns for the nurse. This is when nursing takes on an art form especially in end of life care. That is where awareness of being present, honouring the patient's spiritual being as well as their body is an important aspect of nursing concern.

Once perception is attained the next phase is where knowledge culminates in interpretation.

Interpretive view

Being an expert practitioner,[61] a product of experience, brought about the desire to translate what I learnt. This happened about the time of my career change when I went beyond the received and perceived view of experience. I continued to interpret the situation of those I perceived and discovered that they had 'feelings, ideas, choices and purpose in their individual way of expression'.[62] I developed a level of understanding that illuminated the situation. It not only promoted knowledge building but also increased the way I valued caring ideals.

The main thrust of my study centred on understanding the motivations for moving to end of life nursing care. To understand this I needed to explore avenues that addressed nursing work that I often accepted without thinking about in any serious manner. An illustration of this is the story of Bill whom I hold in high regard among my learning concerns. I nursed him virtually at the end of his life when he could still communicate. He was able then to share stories interspersed with memories of good days. With the help of his family, intimate glimpses of a man of integrity emerged. Bill had a chance to momentarily forget his pain and loneliness. This was a precious commodity not only for Bill and his family, but also for me as his nurse. The experience of facing the change in him at our next meeting was a reminder of how cruel physical deterioration can be:

> *Bill is now deeply unconscious. Tracy (Bill's daughter) somehow lost a lot of the distress she exhibited last week, she is more*

---

61. P Benner, *From Novice To Expert: Excellence And Power In Clinical Nursing Practice* (Upper Saddler River, NJ: Prentice Hall, 2001).
62. Meleis, *Theoretical Nursing*, 495.

> *relaxed. She talks with ease now about her life as each day becomes one to cherish in her father's presence.*

Connectedness at the time of intense grief creates a warm climate at the bedside. This is a time when all are open and honest, forgiving and generous. Bill's family was no exception. They prayed together and I prayed with them.

> *I touched Bill gently and felt a connectedness. Connectedness that is difficult to explain in context of a scientific model. Touching Bill's forehead relaxed the lines that were signatures of the discomfort he suffered. Leaving my hand in place I sensed his breathing slow down to a comfortable pace. At the same time I had an acutely perceptible sensation of peace leaving me comforted as well.*

My hand on Bill's head felt warm. The rest of my body gradually relaxed as Bill's facial muscles smoothed and his breathing slowed. Eyes closed, a barely perceptible smile on his lips gave me the answer. I have done my work well. Bill was not in pain and I left quietly. Another day:

> *Bill's wife said: 'He is comfortable because he knows you are here'. Did I connect with him? I must have done so with my presence. Did he want that presence? He was too sick to tell me, but his face relaxed when I touched him. Was it because his family was relaxed and I was seen to be responsible for his comfort? I took his hand and held it. I let him hold on and willed myself to be with him fully. Had he been able to tell me that he is dying he would have known that I have accepted it. He could have made a deliberate connection with me in his subconscious and I promised to be there at the end.*

Was all this possible because I am comfortable with end of life situations? Did Bill in the throws of dying sense that? Could it be that my manner and 'quiet practice' is what a dying person looks for? Bill will never be able to tell me. Was the instinctive recall of my personal experience with death the key to understanding this grieving family?

I would like to answer these questions by talking about how I interpret situations occurring in my palliative caring. It takes my background of clinical experience with seriously ill patients to explore how I am able to interpret the unsaid words.

8. Consciousness: the patient and the nurse's knowledge building

Interpreting silent messages from this dying man was enabled by my conscious observation and engagement of my reflectivity,[63] the ontological thread of my 'deep humanitarian outlook… within the unfolding moment'.[64] This at times surprised me because it happened without conscious preparation.

Recall of Parse's theoretical principles adds further to my understanding of the acute sensitivity of the meaning and recognition of the pivotal experience with Bill. Parse speaks of:

1. Structuring meaning through valuing and imaging reality;
2. Co-creating patterns while relating to life even if it is paradoxical;
3. Co-transcending 'while forge[ing] unique paths with shifting perspectives as a different light is cast on the familiar'.[65]

Yes, I sensed Bill's comfort, related to his position in the end of his existence and co-transcended some of the way with him.

The other nursing theory complementing my understanding is 'health as expending consciousness' developed by Margaret Newman that sees health and illness as expanding consciousness over the vista of human existence. Newman as a young woman was the sole carer of her mother who was suffering a debilitating neurological disease. In that time, her mother's 'illness reflected the life pattern of the person',[66] that she later as a nurse recognised and accepted. That is how Newman came to the conclusion that the the physical approach to health and ageing changes when the meaning of expanding consciousness is applied to them. Newman's theory of expanding consciousness does

---

63. C Johns, *Engaging Reflection In Practice* (Oxford: Blackwell Publishing, 2006).
64. C Johns, 'Reflective Practice: Revealing The [He]art Of Caring', in *International Journal of Nursing Practice*, 7 (2001): 237–245.
65. RR Parse, (ed), *Illuminations: The Human Becoming Theory In Practice And Research* (Sudbury: Jones and Bartlett Publishers, 1999).
66. Newman,1994, *Health As Expanding Consciousness*, xx.

not only effect the patient but also the nurses through their 'unitary human[ity]'.[67] Newman's concept works well in unison with Parse's theory as both support a non-fragmentary image of people. A person is seen as a tapestry of beings that function as one holistic entity.[68] Being a thinking being, the nurse reaches a stage in professional practice when revisions of caring values pay dividends. This is often followed by a life changing decision in the concept of wholeness. There will be no separation of physical, emotional or psychological entities. The unitary being of the whole person is involved.

The nurse working with Newman's theory will appreciate the process of 'expansion of consciousness' as it could transform and enhance practice and life. The nurse's working consciousness expands constantly as day-to-day changes in patients' conditions calls for understanding and adaptation. Parse, by advocating human becoming as a constant flow also recognizes 'growth' within a functional life model and advocates an expansion of mind or consciousness.[69]

This mindset or theory adds three further kinds of knowledge to the previously discussed views by enriching the theoretical world of the nurse.[70] The kind of knowledge expounded here speaks of mind, biology and the subtle. These involve sensory and symbolic work that appreciates a new meaning of body and mind. The consciousness as it expands understands that life and mind can prosper, no matter how physically challenged. The theory of health as expanding consciousness encourages nurses instead of seeing only sickness, to find the patient's 'power within' and help them use it 'to evolve toward higher consciousness' enabling a life with all manner of disabilities. This may even include people for whom 'absence of disease and disability is no longer possible'.[71] Expanding consciousness is the theory that maintains that people in all situations can face the future, possibly at a slower pace, while they find their true selves. Newman

---

67. Newman, 1994, *Health As Expanding Consciousness*, xviii.
68. C Picard, and T Mariolis, 2002, 'Praxis As A Mirroring Process: Teaching Psychiatric Nursing Grounded In Newman's Health As Expanding Consciousness', in *Nursing Science Quarterly*, 15/2 (2002): 118–122, E Endo, T Myahara, S Suzuki, and T Ohmasa 2005, 'Partnering Of Researcher And Practising Nurses For Transformative Nursing', in *Nursing Science Quarterly*, 18/2 (2005): 138–145.
69. MA Newman, *Transforming Presence* (Philadelphia: FA Davis Company, 2008).
70. Newman, *Transforming Presence*, 5–6.
71. Newman, *Transforming Presence*.

has developed levels within the theory of expanding consciousness that she calls 'patterns'. Health is the evolving unitary pattern that accepts consciousness as the informational capacity to give it meaning in the human environment because 'health and illness are simply manifestations of fluctuations of the life process'.[72]

Newman's theory of expanding consciousness is the knowledge base I often consider when dealing with palliative care. When people are faced with a life ending diagnosis and access palliative care they don't expect to be taken out of the living world. What they look for is a life worth living while they are slowly dying. There is no welcome mat for reminders of death and dying. Most terminally ill people view themselves as changed persons who may need to live a different way. For me to be there and accompany patients was enticing, especially at the time when I was disillusioned with much of the curing model of medicine and nursing.

The knowledge base of Margaret Newman's theory of expanding consciousness[73] and Rosemary Rizzo-Parse's human becoming theory[74] encouraged me to look at my praxis and wonder if my restlessness and desire to move on could have been the result of clinical apathy and a thirst for change. Parse who accepts free choice of meanings, believes in a 'becoming' phenomenon that coexists and co-operates rhythmically with life and the universe. Newman on the other hand looks at consciousness as a guiding principle of being human. Parse, advocates 'possibilities' as valid assumptions and sees paradox as an unproblematic challenging and problem–solving tool.[75] Both theorists follow on a holistic approach to people's development explicating and implicating the order of human experience.

I now return to the nurse who is a deep thinker and reaches a stage when professional situations create questions. Is there a need to review values and ideals? Is there a need to change?

I am the nurse who faced a life changing decision and embraced it as a unitary concept. There was no separation of physical, emotional or psychological entities, because my unitary being as a whole person was involved in my decision-making. I was conscious of each step.

---

72. Newman, *Transforming Presence*, 6.
73. Newman, *Transforming Presence*.
74. Parse, *Illuminations: The Human Becoming Theory In Practice And Research*.
75. Parse, *Illuminations: The Human Becoming Theory In Practice And Research*, 5–7.

Consciousness played a pivotal role in my every day existence. The more I engaged with Margaret Newman's way of thinking, the more I realised that expanding consciousness does underpin nursing transformation. The nurse working with Newman's theory appreciates the process as it could transform and enhance end of life. Nurses' working consciousness expands constantly as day-to-day changes in the patients' condition call for understanding and adaptation. Parse also advocates human becoming as a constant flow. In fact 'becoming' is actually 'growing' within a functional life model.[76]

It makes sense that the energy of human becoming could easily be linked with 'expansion of human consciousness,'[77] thus marrying the two nursing theories that would illuminate and promote the act of human transformation.

As it happened for me

Now is the time when I need to find what contributed to the transformation of my thinking that endorsed the move to hospice work. This is the main point of the question that develops the study. I am building a case that says how I went through the change that altered my outlook about the basic principle of patient care, how that went from concentrating on a healing process to supporting situations where life was no longer sustainable.

How did it come about, how did I think it through? The first consideration sent me in the direction of care as perceived as a vocation.

Nursing: a vocation that transforms

> *Three workers [were] breaking up rocks. When the first was asked what he was doing, he replied: 'Making little ones out of big ones'; the second said: 'Making a living'; and the third: 'Building a cathedral'.*[78]

---

76. Newman, *Transforming Presence*, 5–8.
77. Newman, *Health As Expanding Consciousness*.
78. JJ Ryan, 'Humanistic Work: Its Philosophical And Cultural Implications', in *A Matter Of Dignity: Inquiries Into The Humanization Of Work*, edited by W

I find it difficult to talk about vocation because I can feel it but the words to express it disappear soon after they come into view. Ryan's citation above describes my quandary in talking of something that has been an integral part of my being as long as I can remember, but no one ever asked why. The men in the quotation above describe the work they were engaged in according to their understanding. They all had a valid answer, but possibly only the third one described his job as a vocation. He had a vision of his place in the scheme of things, in the majesty of a cathedral. I feel comfortable with this man's concept of the way he saw his role in 'breaking up rocks'. This takes me back in time when I started building my own 'cathedral', and met what I later would recognise as the attribute of a 'vocation'.

I now reflect on the evolving model of care that was a part of my person long before I arrived at the door of hospice work. This study is addressing the very reason behind a nursing transformation that was inspired by caring concepts that led to the understanding of human suffering. The best way I can foresee the probable outcome of this study is to talk of the past, present and contemplate the future in a personal style. I need to be auto-ethnographic, to organise the quagmire of experience that was never without lessons learnt. In a way my text is a confession of why care and compassion feature strongly in the story of my life and nursing practice. Evidence of this was there long before palliative care. It was a part of me when I was a teenager and started nursing more than fifty years ago.

Caring as natural ability

The first time I came face to face with sick patients was as a young care worker in an infectious diseases hospital. There I spent extended hours with patients who needed that little extra care. This takes me back to the iron-lung ward of the 1950s where doing the most basic tasks added value to post polio victims' quality of life. After supposedly going off duty I would stay to wash the hair of patients, feed them their favourite snacks or read to them. I was barely seventeen and did not know what I did was a vocational offering.[79] Back then I could not

---

J Heisler and JW Houck, (Notre Dame Ind: University of Notre Dame Press, 1977), 11.

79. M Lundmark, 'Vocation In Theology-Based Nursing Theories', in *Nursing*

explain what directed me. I did not consider helping needy people as work. Later I discovered that 'care' was powering my professional attitude and was at the heart of all that I did. Margaret Bradshaw maintains, 'contents and direction of care have been our nursing heritage'.[80] However at the same time she is concerned that nursing seldom stops to remember that caring is a form of social capital that is slowly losing its value base.

Christopher Johns upholds that while the 'nature of caring' is difficult to pinpoint accurately, by using reflexivity in our work we 'encourage an effective practice'.[81] Caring is a varied observable factor that relies on the individual to balance various dimensions that focus 'on the well-being of the person'.[82] A good illustration reinforcing could be considered the individualistic nature of caring, is by Sundin and Jansson who describe a difficult situation where reciprocity is the focus. In promoting a 'caring' communion with their aphasic patient, they were rewarded with appropriate effective understanding in 'silent dialogue' with one who could not speak.[83] I have experienced similar situation with a person I will call Mary, who was in an 'iron-lung' after polio completely paralysed her. She was totally dependent on the respirator for her existence; without it she would have died because of air hunger. The only way she could communicate her distress when out of the respirator was a clicking noise made with her mouth. I must admit it always scared me when hearing it. I had to respond quickly either using an oxygen mask or putting her back into the iron-lung promptly. Developing what I considered a trusting relationship was the result of my fast reaction that left me, a young inexperienced nurse, with feelings of a job well done. While this was

---

Ethics, 14/ 6 (2007): 767–780; MM Thiel, and S Harris 2005, 'Hope And Vocation', in *The Journal of Supportive Oncology*, 3/3 (2005): 234–5; A Bradshaw, A 1994, *Lighting The Lamp: The Spiritual Dimensions Of Nursing Care*, (London: Scutari, 1994), A Bradshaw, A 1999, 'The Virtue Of Nursing: The Covenant Of Care', in *Journal of Medical Ethics*, 25/66 (1999): 477– 481.

80. A Bradshaw, 'The Spiritual Dimension Of Hospice: The Secularisation Of An Ideal', in *Social Science and Medicine,* 43/3 (1996): 409-419.
81. Johns, 'Reflective Practice: Revealing The [He]art Of Caring', 237.
82. CJ Sabatino, 'Reflections On The Meaning Of Care', in *Nursing Ethics*, 6/5 (1999): 574–582, at 574.
83. K Sundin, and L Jansson, 'Understanding And Being Understood As A Creative Caring Phenomenon In Care Of Patients With Stroke And Aphasia', in *Journal of Clinical Nursing*, 12 (2003): 107–116, at 107.

early in my professional life, it remained a memory that spurred me onto higher caring ideals that formed my vocation, though I rarely thought of that as something special.

Much later when I decided to study my role in the human drama of death and dying, I came to the conclusion that there had to be changes to the caring ideals I knew so well. I had to appraise the way I looked at the value of life without a future and the inevitability of death. Being primarily a clinician my theorising essentially evolved through observational activities of hospice work. I found that nurses in hospice and palliative care were different from nurses in the general wards, where saving lives was the main concern.[84] My transfer to palliative care was significant. It was a radical change from getting patients back to a healthy life to the promotion of a peaceful death. I became anxious to find what contributed to the transformation of vocational thinking that endorsed this move.

It has a long history that started with my introduction to a notion that transformation can be learnt, but I had difficulty with understanding this because transformation for me, the nurse, meant an emotional response to a situation, not an educational process.[85] Whilst I did not question that transformative learning may be a valid way of teaching a theoretical belief, I was not clear of its fittingness for nursing research.[86] Eventually I came to the conclusion after reading Gadamer that change could easily result from experience where 'knowledge . . . is created from interpretations in light of new

---

84. L Barbato-Gaydos, 'The Living End', in *Journal of Hospice and Palliative Care*, 6/1 (2004): 17–26; M Dobratz, 'Hospice Nursing: Presence, Perspectives And Future Directives', in *Cancer Nursing*, 13/ 2 (1990): 16–22; D Hutchings, D 1997, 'The Hardiness Of Hospice Nurses', in *The American Journal of Hospice and Palliative Care*, May-June (1997): 110–113; E Sorensen-Marshall, 2009, 'Margaret Shanks, Nurse to Susan B Anthony: Exploring The Extraordinary In The "Ordinary" Nurse', in *Advances in Nursing Science*, 32/1 (2009): 43–54; DJ Wright, 'Hospice Nursing: The Speciality', in *Cancer Nursing*, 24/1 (2001): 20–27.
85. Parse, *Illuminations: The Human Becoming Theory In Practice And Research*; Endo, et 'Partnering Of Researcher And Practising Nurses For Transformative Nursing';
86. P Cranton and M Roy, 'When The Bottom Falls Out Of The Bucket', *Journal of Transformative Education*, 1 /2 (2003): 86–98; JB Cohen, 'Late For School: Stories For Transformation In An Adult Education Program', in *Journal of Transformative Education*, 2/3 (2004): 242–252.

experience'.[87] For me this signified that whatever the 'new' is I would first reflect on my past that could make me truly 'mindful of myself'.[88]

That is why I reflect critically on how it was when I worked with patients. I recall times when at the bedside I stood back and developed two entities, one the active 'doing' person, and the other who 'watched' that scene with all its nuances. I often imagined myself above looking down. I was seeing more than a bed with a patient and a nurse performing certain tasks. The scene had an energy that directed all actors to play their individual roles.[89] Unconsciously I absorbed tacit, soundless knowledge where earlier there was only acute observation. With each patient contact I went on changing as I immersed myself in a developmental transition [as I now realise]. I went on a constant thinking journey that changed my perceptions of practice. I was encouraged to search for and find my reasons for wanting to be in a changed environment.

Yes, I am certain that the transfer from years of saving lives to supporting people at the end of theirs was surely the result of my tragic personal losses. Perception of my professional goal had changed when I reappraised life and work. I changed my outlook concerning the future like Kendall who witnessed tragedy that promoted change in herself and her environment.[90] I barely got past reading the introduction and literature review of her article when there she was talking about how people react to news of a cancer diagnosis. She spoke of psychological, spiritual and physiological changes in everyone involved in that experience including herself. This was a life-changing event altering everyone's outlook. Everyone in this drama was transformed to a new level of being, never to return to their previous selves.

Change in nursing outlook discussed in literature does not sufficiently explain the auto-ethnographic experience or a radical change from curing care to comfort care.[91] Can a learning process give the rationale for that radical transformation?

---

87. Gadamer, *Truth and Method*, 337.
88. Johns, *Engaging Reflection In Practice*, 4.
89. J Osmond, and Y Darlington, 'Reflective Analysis: Techniques For Facilitating Reflection', in *Australian Social Work,* 58/1 (2005): 3–14.
90. S Kendall, 'Witnessing Tragedy: Nurses' Perceptions Of Caring For Patients With Cancer', in *International Journal of Nursing Practice,* 13 (2007): 111–120.
91. L York and L Sharoff, 'An Extended Epistemology For Fostering Transformative

Elias writes that a learning process is the expansion of consciousness 'through the transformation of world views'.[92] This, in a way agrees with Margaret Newman's theory of health as 'expanding consciousness'. That is that a view where she looks at health care where not only stimulates are concerned for the one for whom complete curing health care is no longer an option, but one that also enhances the nurse's life by transforming it in the process of that change in the emphasis of the care given.[93] Holland-Wade, adopting Newman's model, found that transformation of both patient and nurse happens as the result of their therapeutic relationship.[94] She found that the patients comfort during the interaction promoted a transformative experience for the patient and also for the nurse.

However, for me, the question remains whether 'transformative learning' could explain my change to palliative care nursing. Is it 'learning' that influences the growth of my knowledge base of critical meaning? Is it, according to Erickson, a naturally evolving response to life changes?[95] I found that this may be true in my case because during years of work in health care I discovered that I became more inclusive, discriminating, permeable and integrative of experience and was increasingly conscious of a change that valued my professional status.

The issue remains, what was it that sent me towards palliative care?

Mezirow answers some of this by arguing that transformation is usually prompted by pivotal epiphanic experience, or an 'aha' moment.[96] Cranton clarifies this by adding that transformation is not only a phenomenon that just happens.[97] It involves building knowledge by complementing what is already known. This could then substantiate my use for some transformative learning. It could

---

Learning in Holistic Nursing Education And Practice', in *Holistic Nursing Practice,* 16/1 (2001): 21–29; G Holland-Wade, 'A Concept Analysis Of Personal Transformation', in *Journal of Advanced Nursing,* 28/ 4 (1998): 713.
92. D Elias, D 1997, 'Its Time To Change Our Minds', 3.
93. M Newman, 2006, Health as Expanding Consciousness, Personal Web page, accessed 18.07.2007, http://www.healthexpandingconsciousness.org
94. Holland-Wade, 'A Concept Analysis Of Personal Transformation'.
95. E Erikson, 'The Way Of Looking At Things', in *Personality And Personal Growth, 3rd* third edition, edited by J Fadiman and R Frager, (New York: Harper Collins College Publishers, 1987).
96. Mezirow, *Learning As Transformation.*
97. P Cranton, *Understanding And Promoting Transformative Learning,* second edition, (San Francisco CA: Jossey-Bass, 2006).

explain the experience of my adopting palliative care ideals. Because caring for terminally ill patients not only requires extensive clinical knowledge, but also has room for personal life-experience that promotes better understanding for suffering along side recognition and acceptance of the others' values and beliefs. It can also endorse the ability to transform painful times into emotional growth.[98] To understand what happens to me personally when at the bedside of a dying patient I refer to Parse (1999) when she maintains that transformation is evolutionary.[99]

My day with Shirley is such an example. I was lifted up to new heights that day. I did not consider it work; it was the 'giving' of myself that received more in return.

Shirley

I nursed a special woman. We met approximately two weeks before she died. On that day I was her primary nurse. A week later I wrote a journal entry of the experience.

> *Shirley was a special person because of the way she faced death with full awareness of all that it involved. She had conscious knowledge of where she was going. Shirley and I built a special relationship during the all too brief period that followed our meeting. I am grateful for having been responsible in easing her distressing physical symptoms and enabling her to face the end in relative comfort.*
>
> *The spreading cancerous growth blocked both of her tubes leading from the kidneys to her bladder. The preceding months had seen Shirley have several surgical procedures to enable continuity of kidney functions.*
>
> *Before her admission to the hospice however she opted for comfort care only, no more surgical intervention, no more drastic measures to save her life. Shirley was ready to die. Being*

---

98. B Johnston and LN Smith. 2005, 'Nurses And Patients' Perceptions Of Expert Palliative Nursing Care', in *Journal of Advanced Nursing*, 54/6 (2005): 700–709; MH Kehoe, 'Embodiment Of Hospice Nurses: A Meta-Synthesis Of Qualitative Studies', in *Journal of Hospice and Palliative Nursing*, 8/3 (2006): 137–146, M Newman, *Health As Expanding Consciousness;* DJ Wright, 'Hospice Nursing: The Speciality', in *Cancer Nursing*, 24/1 (2001): 20–27.
99. Parse, *Illuminations*.

a nurse she knew what that decision meant but she had no wish to continue living life that was only a bare 'existence'. What she had forgotten was the extent of the physical suffering as the kidneys gave up their useful life.

Her final two days brought untold pain and distress that only medical intervention and increased medications made somewhat bearable. The drugs made her sleepy but without them she was in severe distress. Only her keen intellect and strong will made possible the final communications and goodbyes. Shirley was single by choice but the many friends, siblings, nieces and nephews atoned for the family and children she never had.

Shirley and I had many conversations during which we shared life experience and dreams. All this was made possible by the time it took to attend to her physical needs. Making her comfortable in a clean bed with many of the small caring treats offered excellent opportunity to get to know Shirley the human being behind the ravages of the diseased body.

Of all the days I shared with her the one when she died was the most memorable. After a restless night and much medication Shirley was difficult to understand in the morning when I took over her care. She tried to tell me something that clearly worried her. Her speech was slurred; it took me some time sitting by her side to make sense of what she was trying to ask me. She must have sensed that her time was up and was anxious to talk of her last wish. By holding her hand, gently stroking her head I managed to get her to relax by indicating that I had time to stay.

Gradually Shirley explained that she wanted me to ring an interstate nephew who did not know how sick she was. She wanted me to let him know that the old prayer book she promised to get restored had not been completed. I worked out a solution with her niece to carry out this task. Shirley, visibly calm now, asked for more pain relief, then went to sleep never to wake. The time following Shirley's death was special. I had an opportunity to meet her extended family and friends as they came and went. Stopping to sit with Shirley, talking with each other reliving memories. Her special friend, also called Shirley, eased the burden of notifying all relevant people about her death. That task usually falls to the nurse.

Looking back, reflecting on this experience I had to rethink what enabled this special relationship with a dying patient, a connectedness that is such an important element of hospice nursing.

> *I slowly came to the conclusion that I needed to build trust.*
>
> *Shirley, herself a nurse, was familiar with not only the medical approach but all the comfort care that was so important when seriously sick, care that did not only consist of a clean comfortable bed, diet as she wished, appropriate opportunity for elimination but also the way that was delivered. The nurse caring for the dying person needs to be polite, gentle and patient. Never rushing, always ensuring that the patient's wishes are carried out.*
>
> *I felt comfortable with Shirley the way she did with me. All her wishes were important and I made certain that they got priority attention. Any question she addressed to me was answered honestly and those I was unsure of I followed up and communicated at a later date. Any changes proposed in treatment I discussed with Shirley before they were implemented and if she had any objections her wishes were observed. I believe that earning Shirley's trust was the key player of our relationship. I made certain that I respected her extensive nursing and medical knowledge and I hoped that at no time did I behave in a patronising manner. I expected the same treatment towards her from all others who cared for her.*

Shirley's story made me ask why I responded to her so readily and effectively. For me there was no need to think about what to do, it just happened. I knew what to do. However later, when I stopped and thought it through, I realised that intuition derived from previous knowledge let me do the right thing. 'Complex interaction of attributes'[100] could have contributed to my actions. I engaged a synergy of factors such as nursing knowledge and clinical experience that promoted a response without hesitation creating a transformative evolution of ideals. Nursing terminally ill people contributes awareness on multiple levels of complex care situations. I often used what I best could call 'gut feelings' where I instinctively knew what to do.[101] When opportunity later allowed me to think it through I found

---

100. HH McCuthcheon and J Pincombe, 'Intuition: An Important Tool In The Practice Of Nursing', in *Journal of Advanced Nursing*, 35/5 (2001): 342–348 at 345
101. MM Kosowski and W Roberts, 'When Protocols Are Not Enough: Intuitive Decision Making By Novice Nurse Practitioners', in *Journal of Holistic Nursing*, 21/1 (2003): 52–72 at 58.

that I could name the exact knowledge base I used for the action. All that could have come from momentary recall of a similar situation urging me to act. I depended on experience as therapeutic ideals to suit the present action that often transformed my caring approach.[102]

I now refer briefly to how I understand the concept of vocation that could foreshadow transformation. This for me remains still a question in the case of this study.

Vocation: does it promote transformation?

Definitions of vocation vary but in essence most authors make similar key observations. Michael Collins believes that vocation 'refers to a calling [that is a] firm commitment to the performance of worthwhile activities [and] nothing is worthwhile for a human being which he or she cannot do with passionate devotion'.[103] Thiel and Harris[104] write how clinicians in the early career enter with a strong sense of vocation and adopt Buechner's definition that reads as 'the place where your deep gladness meets the world's deep needs'.[105] Eliot in Mintz believes that: 'true calling . . . [is] asserting one's unique individuality . . . apart from work or wealth accumulation',[106] while White argues, 'that [the] nursing vocation is motivation that encourages responses for the sake of the patient'.[107] Counselling psychologists Dik and Duffy's definition comes closest to how I understand vocational concepts. They maintain that:

---

102. JA Effken, 'The Informational Basis For Nursing Intuition: Philosophical Underpinnings', in *Nursing Philosophy*, 8 (2007): 187–200; L King and JV Appleton, 'Intuition: A Critical Review Of The Research And Rhetoric, in *Journal of Advanced Nursing*, 26 (1997): 194–202; Kosowski and Roberts, 'When Protocols Are Not Enough'; LA Ruth-Sahd and EJ Tisdell, 'The Meaning And Use Of Intuition In Novice Nurses: A Phenomenological Study', in *Adult Education Quarterly*, 57/2 (2007): 115–140.
103. M Collins, *Adult Education as Vocation* (New York: Routledge, 1991), 40–42.
104. MM Thiel and S Harris 'Hope And Vocation', in *The Journal of Supportive Oncology*, 3/3 (2005): 234–5.
105. F Buechner, *Wishful Thinking: A Seeker's ABC* (New York: Harper Collins Publishers, 1993), 234.
106. A Mintz, *George Eliot & The Novel On Vocation* (Harvard: Harvard University Press, 1978), 34.
107. K White, 'Nursing As Vocation', in *Nursing Ethics*, 9/3 (2002): 284.

> *A vocation is an approach to a particular life role that is oriented toward demonstrating or deriving a sense of purpose or meaningfulness and that holds other-oriented values and goals as primary sources of motivation.*[108]

This brings home to me why I so often did not see myself as 'working,' because to me being with patients was my role and gave purpose to my professional existence. I believe though that work can be a calling or vocation in any type of activity. Anyone who conscientiously conducts a work role could have satisfaction even without financial rewards, because work for them is a vocation.[109] This last statement spoke closely to why I rarely thought of being rewarded while I was with patients. Sick and dying people in a comfortable bed, pain free and resting was my payment.

Putting my energy into the care of terminally ill patients directed my final vocational development. Specific experiential signposts directed that career choice. Witnessing death at an early age and going on to further personal losses, determined my ability to understand 'others' in their grief. My choice for end of life situations came at a late point and I remained with it for twenty years, way past the time when the general population of nurses retire from active work. The value of having the opportunity to witness and share intimate moments at the end of people's lives has enriched my own immeasurably. In the process of reflecting on this I evaluated what I have achieved in my nursing career and what that meant to the profession and myself. This is when with clarity of vision I became fully conscious of the transformation.

This understanding of vocation and transformation now leads me to talk about the culture of palliative medicine and nursing as an evolving health care specialty. The following section will not only talk about the concept but will also introduce special people who are responsible for promoting care of terminally ill patient care.

---

108. BJ Dik and RD Duffy, 'Calling And Vocation At Work: Definition And Prospects For Research And Practice', in *The Counselling Psychologist*, 37/3 (2008): 424–450, at 428.
109. Dik and Duffy, 'Calling And Vocation At Work'.

9. Hospice and palliative care: aa historical review

> *The resilience of those who continue to work in this field is won by full understanding of what is happening and not by a retreat behind a technique.*[110]

Nursing had a special place in my life. I always knew that I wanted to be with frail and sick persons. I knew there was a place for me somewhere where people were in need of care. It was not an easy dream to fulfil. During hospital training when severe military obedience overshadowed caring aspirations I nearly lost the spirit I took with me into training. I nearly turned my back on bullying and contemptible treatment by giving in to the feeling of failure. I am speaking here of the early 1950s when the sister in charge of the ward and matron of the hospital behaved like an army sergeant major. I lost faith in the system but the sick patients in the uncomfortable beds kept me there, in spite of the strict regimented treatment that I endured for three years. The years of bullying did not persuade me to give up because what mattered was the patient in the bed. It was a type of 'giving' without expecting a return. I wanted to serve people who needed service, who were in a position of helpless confusion, when the bodily functions were in disarray, when illness and suffering turned lives upside down. I remained with it and gained experience in various fields until deciding to choose caring for terminally ill patients. My joining the palliative care/hospice field was a conscious decision of the experienced nurse who by then had not only clinical expertise but also extensive life experience. The desire to give more than medicalised care urged me to new challenges where the whole person care mattered. Palliative care and hospice nursing responded to this. Promoting quality of life for those who were dying became my aim.

It was interesting that while involved in clinical patient care at the bedside, I had little or no desire to find out where this specialty started or who the pioneers of palliative management were. In my experience most clinicians plying their palliative care trade were

---

110. C Saunders, 'Hospices', in *Dictionary of Medical Ethics*, edited by AS Duncan, CR Dunstan and RB Welbourne, (London: Dartman Longman and Todd, 1981).

not really concerned where it came from. We were mostly interested in the effect of symptom management and emotional care of patients. We learnt to set up syringe drivers that delivered various medications; we became experienced in evaluating effectiveness of the medications and concentrated on the latest comfort measures. They were the important day-to-day problems that we focused on mainly. We also managed the grief of patients and their families. The work was physically and emotionally demanding and at the end of the day general fatigue sent us home. As we headed out the door we rarely if ever talked about historical aspects. Conversation was mainly about the immediate problems of our patients, the practical aspects of the work and what to cook for dinner that night when we reach home. I am almost certain that if I asked my colleagues today who first introduced regular opiate medication for cancer pain, the answer would be a resounding 'I don't know', followed by 'why does that matter anyway?' I personally always concentrated on the practicality of alleviating the many distressing symptoms of serious illness, until embarking on this research when I realised that palliative care did not happen overnight. There was a history behind it where medical and nursing professionals' combined their effort to build the specialty into a world-wide end of life health management phenomenon. That is why I now ask what the history of palliative care in Western nursing, or indeed of International nursing is? I also want to know how that history impacted on my work, and how historical data could explain the development of the care I adopted for the patients in the hospice?

10. Palliative care: the ideology and practice

> *Bob is not so good today. It is not physical really. It is the loss of his life that he is grieving and that is what he finds difficult to share. However today while making his bed my hand was tightly gripped as he slowly admitted why he is feeling particularly lost and disheartened. He is frightened of dying. I was with him quietly respecting his dignity and patiently listening without much verbal response. Thankfully he settled down to sleeping peacefully and died a few hours later.*

The approach that is used to improve quality of life associated with life threatening illness is known as palliative care.[111] The name for the care of dying people developed from a simple word that means to cloak or shield. The word 'palliation' comes from the Latin *pallium* and means 'shielding the weak'.[112]

Palliative care is a response to people's suffering in the presence of a terminal illness, and is said to be 'a basic human right when curative care is no longer appropriate'.[113] The World Health Organization emphasises provision of quality for the patient's remaining life whether in hospital, home or nursing home.

Theory and practice of palliative care originates from the hospice philosophy of caring for patients with life limiting illness and goes back to the Middle Ages where the philosophy of a good death is believed to have originated from.[114] The name hospice comes from the Latin *hospitium* meaning guesthouse where weary travellers and sick people rest during a journey.[115] Initially religious orders, on route to holy shrines established these intermittent resting places and called them a 'hospice' where the pilgrims, often very ill, would either recover or die at the place of arrival. The sixteenth to the eighteenth centuries saw religious orders of Catholic nuns and brothers offer this care but on the whole most people died in their own home. Later, in France, Jean Garnier established the first dedicated public hospices in the nineteenth century. This young woman lost her two children and husband within a few months of each other and that devastating experience led her to establish several places called *Hotels-Dieu* [God's Hostels]. Jean continued her work in the spirit of the religious pioneers of hospice care looking after dying people.[116]

---

111. World Health Organisation's definition of palliative care, on line, accessed 23.5.2012, http://whqlibdoc.who./hq/2003/WHO_CDS_STB_2003.22.pdf
112. B Johnston, 'Overview Of Nursing Developments In Palliative Care', in *Palliative care: the nursing role,* (edited by J Lugton and M Kidle, (London: Churchill Livingston, 2002), 1.
113. D Doyle, G Hanks, and N MacDonald, 'Introduction', in *The Oxford Textbook of Palliative Medicine*, second edition, edited by D Doyle, G Hanks and N MacDonald (Oxford: Oxford University Press, Oxford, 2003).
114. F Randall and RS Downey, *Philosophy of Palliative Care* (Oxford: Oxford University Press, 2006).
115. WebMD on line viewed 23.5.2012, http://www.webmd.com/search/search_results/default.aspx?query=Hospice
116. M Salamagne, 'Hospice in France', in *Hospice Care On The International Scene,*

Mary Aikenhead, an Irish Sister of Charity, opened the first Our Lady's Hospice in Dublin in 1879 that she dedicated exclusively to the care of dying people. From Ireland the hospice work expanded to Great Britain in several municipalities and charitably funded places that were staffed by religious carers. Of these in the early 1900s St Luke's Hospice and the Hospice of God in London are noted to have focused on the so-called dying destitute population.

In the 1980s hospice principles were slowly recognised and eventually embraced by the medical profession and became known as hospice and palliative care services.[117]

Pioneers of note

The palliative care approach is a widely accepted method of treatment for people with life limiting illness now but it was not always so. It all began with the determination of Cicely Saunders to make a difference in the life of people with terminal illness by influencing the treatment of this vulnerable group of sick people. Saunders went on to inspire others such as Elizabeth Kubler-Ross in the USA, Dr Balfour-Mount in Canada and Dr Murray-Parkes in the UK who, among others, started the palliative care movement.

Dame Cicely Saunders – Britain

Dr Cicely Saunders is credited with being the pioneer who formally introduced care of terminally ill people and called it palliative care. She initially trained as a nurse in wartime London at St Thomas' Hospital where she worked in various nursing specialties. Late in her training a back injury put an end to her future in nursing even after graduating with honours. Saunders had to find an alternative career path. This led her to qualifying in social work. For some years she held the position of Almoner at St Thomas Hospital's Northcote Trust, an organisation that specialised in the care of cancer patients. Saunders by that time also completed a course in cancer nursing at the Royal Cancer Hospital and wanted to remain in that field. In

---

edited by C Saunders and R Kastenbaum, (New York: Springer Publishing Company, 1997).
117. Saunders and Kastenbaum, *Hospice Care On The International Scene.*

the meantime while she felt at ease in her almoner's role, Saunders missed the connection with dying patients and yearned to return to nursing and try to make a difference. Dr Norman Barret a surgeon with whom she worked suggested that as a nurse she would not be listened to and suggested to 'Go and read medicine. It is the doctors who desert the dying. There is so much more to learn about pain'. He meant that the difference Saunders craved needed to start with the doctors.[118] As a mature age student Saunders graduated in medicine with research in pain management an added qualification.

This was when she converted to Christianity. That pleased and confused her at the same time and left her spending many hours praying for an understanding of where her life should lead.[119] Saunders eventually developed her individual reaction to the loneliness and isolating power of death, giving her incentive towards founding a hospice, where people were not left to die alone.[120]

In 1967 Dr Saunders opened St Christopher's Hospice in London embracing a multi-disciplinary approach to the care of dying patients. She was the first medical practitioner who promoted regular administration of drugs to control physical pain. She paid careful attention to spiritual and psychological suffering of not only the patient but also of the family. Dr Saunders was the first person to promote palliative care as a way to treat end of life issues in a scientific way adding an existential aspect of caring at the same time. She in fact pioneered a new dimension in medicine.[121]

Dr Elizabeth Kubler-Ross – United States of America

In the 1960s Kubler-Ross a Swiss psychiatrist became interested in society's response to terminal illness through her physician husband at the University of Chicago Medical School. She formulated and published her theories on the subject of death and dying, and was responsible for setting up seminars initially for students of medicine,

---

118. Saunders and Kastenbaum, *Hospice Care On The International Scene*, 4.
119. S DuBoulay, *Cecily Saunders: Founder Of The Modern Hospice Movement* (London: Hodder and Stoughton, 1984).
120. L Thoresen, 'A Reflection On Cicely Saunders' Views On A Good Death Through The Philosophy Of Charles Taylor', in *International Journal of Palliative Nursing*, 9/1 (2003): 19-23.
121. DuBoulay, *Cecily Saunders*.

sociology and psychology and later for nurses and relatives of patients. Publishing her best-selling book, *On Death and Dying*,[122] encouraged significant interest in the subject. Drs Kubler-Ross and Saunders were responsible for the founding of the first hospice in the United States of America. This came about through Ed Dobihal the Director of Religious Ministries at New Haven Hospital in Yale. He heard Kubler-Ross speak of Cicely Saunders' work and that encouraged him to contact Dr Saunders and the rest is history.[123]

Dr Balfour-Mount – Canada

In January 1973 Dr Balfour Mount attended a seminar given by Elizabeth Kubler-Ross where she discussed her book, *On Death and Dying,* urging him to action. He invited an interested group of doctors to discuss the Kubler-Ross publication. Mount believed that as a surgeon dealing with cancer patients he would know all about the subject of death and dying, but was surprised to find that he knew very little. The discussion group became interested in Kubler-Ross' findings of terminally ill patients being shunned, their pain ignored and left to die in agony by the medical profession. Balfour-Mount decided to research the pain aspect and was astounded at the inadequacy of care for dying people in flagship hospitals of North America like Montreal's teaching institution The Royal Victoria Hospital. Mount then visited St Christopher's Hospice on Cicely Saunders' invitation. On returning to Canada he created a hospice like ward at the Royal Victoria hospital making that unit then the birth of palliative care in North America. By the end of the 1970s Dr Mount gave up surgery and devoted the rest of his medical life to this newly formed end of life caring specialty. He had some difficult times but he was now in his twilight when years he found that he was considered the father of palliative care in Canada.[124]

---

122. E Kubler-Ross, *On Death And Dying* (London: Tavistock Publications, 1969).
123. M O'Rawe-Amenta, 'Holism, Hospice And Nursing', in *Nursing Care Of The Terminally Ill,* edited by M O'Rawe-Amenta and NL Bohnet (Boston: Little, Brown and Company, 1986).
124. The Ottowa Citizen, April 25, 2005, 'A moral force: the story of Dr Balfour-Mount' on line, viewed on 18.05.11, http://www.canada.com/ottawacitizen/story.html?id=896d005a-fedd-4f50-fedd-a2d9-83a95fc56464

Dr Colin Murray-Parks

As an eight-year-old Colin knew what he wanted to do with his life; he wanted to be a doctor. He became interested in Psychiatry even before entering university. While completing his medical training at Westminster Hospital he became intrigued by medicine's failure to address the psychological aspects of human mortality. This made him determined to stay with psychiatry as his chosen profession. Bereavement studies had become a part of his interest since 1959 and led to a long career in grief management and the authorship of publications concerning bereavement studies. Joining the Tavistock Institute of Human Relations (1962–75) encouraged him to develop theories of 'loss and change' in disasters when loss of body parts was a problem. Later as Director of the Harvard Bereavement Project, he met Cicely Saunders who invited him to be Honorary Consultant Psychiatrist at St Christopher's where he is to this day. He was made an Officer of the Order of the British Empire in 1996 for his services to bereaved people.[125]

These four leaders

These four leaders are largely responsible for initiating what today is a global service supporting those whose lives are terminated by disease at any age. Palliative care theory and practice has developed in the Western World since 1976 when St Christopher's brought together a publication that was called 'Essentials for Hospice'.[126] Dr Saunders notes that it is indeed remarkable how hospice and palliative care norms spread to innumerable places in the world through this publication and other initiatives. She adds that with this has also come at the same time a growth in the demand for euthanasia and physician assisted suicide. She called for acceptance of palliative care management for a broader patient population beside cancer.[127] At this stage it became clear that palliative care needed an organising body that would embrace not only palliative care but also approaches

---

125. Saunders and Kastenbaum, *Hospice Care On The International Scene*.
126. Saunders and Kastenbaum, *Hospice Care On The International Scene*.
127. World Health Organisation History, Projects, Structure 2012, on line, accessed 23.5.2012, http://en.wikipedia.org/wiki/World_Health_Organisation

to support diseases in all phases of care in the terminally ill phase and disease generally. The United Nations at its formation in 1945 discussed setting up a global health organisation that came into being three years later.

The World Health Organisation (WHO)

WHO is the directing and coordinating body of health matters within the United Nation's system. It sets norms and standards for evidence based health policies. WHO's constitution came into force on April 7th 1948 and since then this date has been celebrated each year as World Health Day.[128] WHO has programs for various health related issues amongst them approaches to cancer detection, prevention, treatment and palliative care. WHO defined palliative care as the guiding norm for nursing and medicine concerned with life limiting illness problems.[129] WHO maintains that palliative care is an essential part of cancer control and as such can be provided relatively simply and inexpensively. In most of the third world the majority of cancer patients are in advanced stages of the disease when first seen by a medical professional. For them, the only realistic treatment option is pain relief and palliative care. The WHO 'ladder for cancer pain' is a relatively inexpensive yet effective method for relieving pain in about ninety per cent of patients.[130]

By stipulating management of physical and psychological care, WHO reinforces the importance of affirming life and regarding death as a normal process by neither hastening nor postponing death. The WHO's palliative care approach is adopted globally and is the template for training nursing and medical professionals. A major feature of physical and psychological care is the appropriate administration of medicines. The 'Essential Medicines List' documents all medications it deems essential to appropriate palliative patient symptom management in all parts of the world.[131] In 1998 the WHO added guidelines for palliative medication in its 'Essential Medicines List

---

128. World Health Organisation's definition of palliative care, on line, accessed 23.5.2012, http://whqlibdoc.who./hq/2003/WHO_CDS_STB_2003.22.pdf
129. World Health Organisation's definition of palliative care.
130. World Health Organisation's definition of palliative care.
131. World Health Organisation's definition of palliative care.

for Children' with terminal illness, an extensive documentation of all physical symptom-managing agents impacting on young and very young patients.[132]

Hospice and palliative care world-wide: a brief overview

Earlier I expanded on how palliative care evolved from hospice work over decades, even centuries. Those responsible for gradually setting up more intense and somewhat scientific approaches to caring for seriously ill people were medical and nurse practitioners in the specialty of palliative care, initially working from Europe and North America. The driving force behind the first hospice service was Dr Cicely Saunders of Great Britain.[133] Dr Balfour-Mount, her contemporary in Canada, followed by coining the term 'palliative care' and by pioneering the Canadian hospice movement in 1973. As it happened the first International Congress for the Care of the Terminally ill patient was held in Montreal and organised biannually by Balfour -Mount there after. A nurse took the next important step in North America. Florence Wald Dean of Yale Nursing School attended an address by Cecily Saunders at the University of Yale in 1969 leading her to work for a brief period in St Christopher's Hospice. From there she brought back the principles of palliative care. In 1971 Wald established Hospice Inc. in the United States. Hospice care in the United States grew to become a significant part of the health care system. Between 1990 and 2000 over 3000 hospice and palliative care services were introduced in the USA, and in 2008 1.45 million people and their families received hospice care.

In 1980 Dr Josèfina Magno an oncologist, was instrumental in forming the Academy of Hospice and Palliative Medicine in the USA. This led her to set up the International Hospice Institute with Canada that by 1999 evolved into the International Association for Hospice and Palliative Care. By 2008 the IAHPC with Magno as the head of a board of directors from as far afield as Scotland, Argentina, Hong Kong and Uganda successfully expanded the philosophy of palliative care in the member countries.

---

132. Hospice Education Institute on line viewed 15.05.2011, http://www.hospiceworld.org/history.htm
133. DuBoulay, *Cecily Saunders*

Palliative care is well established in Australia and New Zealand. This part of the world followed in the footsteps of Dame Cicely Saunders while establishing the service of hospice and palliative care. Education of nurses has been underway for sometime by nurse academics who lead contemporary clinical and research fields. Among them are Professor Margaret O'Connor, head of Palliative Care Australia, Professor Patsy Yates at Queensland University of Technology and the developer of the Specialist Palliative Care Competencies for Nurses, and Professor Sanchia Aranda, researcher in cancer and palliative care. Australia now has several university programs for palliative care nurse education and Medical Schools include palliative care as a course that can be taken electively.

In Asia the situation also changed. Korea had a hospice service provided by the Little Company of Mary nuns in their Calvary Hospice with services that increased to 60 by 1999. In Japan a hospice service has been provided by Yodogawa Christian Hospital since 1973. The protocol of the WHO's Analgesic Ladder, was introduced to China in 1991, and as a result in 2002 it was said that hundreds of palliative care services sprung up in urban areas.

Africa has a serious problem with terminal illness of which HIV AIDS is by far the major component. Hospice and palliative care services, often supported by external donors, exist in Uganda, Kenya South Africa and Zimbabwe. The newly formed African Palliative Care Association has much potential because the need for palliative care was never more urgent.

After establishment of St Christopher's hospice it took the rest of Europe ten years to catch up. After 1990 there was rapid expansion of palliative care in most countries. In 1989 and 1992 the European Parliament actually adopted resolutions to provide counselling and care of terminally ill people but showed little interest in other end of life issues. In 2005 again questions were asked but no noticeable changes were noted.

My palliative care

Palliative care nursing comes to life in the following two stories. The first one is hypothetical, inspired by a colleague who wondered what I meant by saying that without control of physical symptoms, existential and emotional problems could become unmanageable. I decided to write a tale that is based on my actual experience with patients over the years. The second is communication between a patient and myself that took place on night duty in the hospice.

Pain that suddenly changes

It all began in a doctor's consulting rooms where the doctor had just told a patient that the pain she endured for months would actually kill her. Suddenly she is paralysed with fear, she cannot move, disbelieving, she only stares at the doctor. I am going to call the patient 'Jill'.

> *The problem that the doctor has been investigating for some weeks by now is caused by invasive liver cancer. Jill was overcome by the increased intensity of the pain since he told her that he could do no more to help her. She is going to die sooner rather than later. She could not understand how the pain that bothered her for months can become like knives battering her body all of a sudden. His words still hammer her eardrum and her body is burning up with pain. The doctor writes a prescription for morphine and ushers her out into the waiting room where the receptionist stands helplessly. The receptionist tries to reassure Jill that she will be better after she collects the medication downstairs in the pharmacy and takes two of the tablets. That is when Jill overhears the doctor as he books a bed for her in the hospice. She sits down in the nearest chair and begins to sob.*
>
> *Activity in the hospice.*
> *Another busy morning! The usual commotion is in full swing. There are nurses rushing from patient to patient, doctors calling for help and the phone rings incessantly. Eventually someone has time to pick up the receiver and listen to the doctor's voice booking an emergency admission. Yes, it is all about Jill and the problem at the surgery. A bed is allocated for her and a nurse is asked to get ready for the new patient. It is interesting how she does not get ruffled but quietly puts a hot blanket on the bed that will be Jill's.*
>
> *Soon, the paramedics quietly wheel the stretcher in to the hospice with the new patient.*
>
> *There is little time for reading the doctor's notes that pale distressed Jill brought with her. She looks scared, tightly clutching her middle. The paramedics have no history of unusual*

observations aside from the signs of distressing pain. The nurse takes over. She quietly puts Jill into the clean crisp bed with the hot blanket, gives her a hot pack that is put on the painful area, takes readings of temperature, pulse and respiration and sits down to listen to whatever this distressed woman has to say. There is no conversation really, Jill's only activity is to beat her abdomen and scratch her sides. The nurse is mystified but surely there must be something she could do! The solution is clear. Jill needs something to ease the pain; it is obvious that this is more than the woman can endure. A quick call to the doctor results in an order for pain relief quickly administered and Jill soon curls up in the foetal position and goes to sleep. This will do for now but does Irene, the nurse looking after Jill, know anything about her patient's problem? There was no communication and while Jill is comfortable the nurse has no idea who she is caring for apart from a wreck of a human being who now snores and occasionally twitches.

This is the problem of the vicious cycle of pain management.

Physical symptoms were eased to the detriment of finding out why the sudden response to the doctor's information in the office was followed by a tirade of crying and uncontrollable shaking.

This happens when there is a one-way response to a situation.

This is where the cycle begins.

Jill had some pain before. The pain was her companion for some months but she coped. Results of the scan that the doctor shared with Jill shook her to the core. She was told that her disease will kill her and Jill is helpless in the face of all that it implies. The situation in the consulting room was not helped by the receptionist's ignorance of coping with a distressed patient. So the obvious remedy had to be sedation.

Jill will sleep now but when she wakes she will need the expertise of a nurse who has the ability to understand her and have patience to listen.

What I want to illustrate with this example is the reality of physical and emotional pain happening at the same time. The two pain modes are very real to the patient, and management requires two different approaches.

Jill has been suffering and no one can deny that. The question is whether the suffering is physical or emotional or both?

The nurse, especially in hospice and palliative care work, looks at the patient as a whole. Thus s/he will inspect all aspects of the human condition s/he has in the new patient in the bed. The patient the nurse sees in the bed is a human being, a physical body of a heart, lungs, body organs, muscles, bones and tissues but is also a composite of a history a past, one of thoughts, insights, emotions and desires.

What the nurse may do when Jill wakes, by using their skills, presence and gentle communication, is assess the patient. S/he will try and dispel doubts that Jill could have had about the environment. The nurse may, through listening, quietly open a channel of communication where Jill can talk about the anxiety she is feeling and start voicing the meaning she attaches to her pain. Jill may well verbalise her loss of integrity and the threat of disintegration that the doctor's information initiated. It may even be possible that the excruciating pain she suffered in the doctor's consulting room will ease. It is to a large extent up to the nurse and how s/he deals with the situation.

This is a situation that one confronts all too often in the palliative care world, the hospice. The nurse, without conscious awareness, would tap into her/his intuitive knowledge base that told her/him what actions were necessary and how to access the patient and the situation.[134] It takes years of clinical experience to acquire appropriate knowledge that is the hallmark of the expert practitioner promoting intuitive abilities.

The 'vicious' cycle of pain management is illustrated by this story. Jill, without effective physical pain management, could remain distressed and possibly even depressed. However, a chemical/drug/medication only management could possibly leave Jill at the mercy of drugs only. It takes careful balancing of medical and non-medical interventions to attain a beneficial outcome as this incident demonstrates, where both treatment-approaches are advisable.

The nurse in a palliative care situation closely observes the patient as a whole, noting all symptoms and aspects of the composite picture which makes up each patient. The patient has both physical and emotional insight that need to be addressed.

I now follow with the story that actually happened.

---

134. M Polanyi, *The Tacit Dimension*.

One night in the hospice

Knowledge underlining palliative care philosophy rests with understanding and interpreting the multiple situations the nurse encounters in end of life care. These may be family problems, communication issues or symptom management. To illustrate what I mean let me share my real-life meeting one night with a patient I will call 'Joy'.

> *Ringing of the call bell coming from Joy's room interrupted the peaceful quiet of the night. I responded immediately. Entering the dimly lit room I hear an urgent whisper coming from the bed: 'It really hurts. Please do something.' The voice is clipped and angry urging me to act fast. In the dim night-light I see a woman with screwed up face breathing heavily.*
>
> *'Do give me a bolus, a break through injection [extra medication] please!'*
>
> *My right hand finds one of her hands, and gently touching it I say that I am there to help. I do not know Joy and as yet I have not read her medication orders either. Joy soon tells me that the syringe driver at her side is where she gets the bolus from and how much she has each time she presses it. There is no time to look at her medication orders. My skill management of this equipment is a little rusty, which does not help, but with Joy's occasional instructions we both manage to get through this.*
>
> *'It is working', came the soft comment while Joy searched for my nametag to see my name.*
>
> *'I am Susan', I say. 'What shall I call you?'*
>
> *'Joy, Joyce I don't mind.'*
>
> *'How is the pain now?'*
>
> *'Much better. You are the best nurse in this hospital,' she said. I responded with a quiet thank you as she closed her eyes and went to sleep.*
>
> *Before leaving the room I made sure that the call bell was in Joy's hand and dim the light above the bed. The sound of regular breathing follows me down the corridor to the front desk where I catch up on Joy's medication orders and record the bolus I had given. I was glad it was the correct dosage.*

Returning to the desk I thought about Joy. Somehow I had a warm feeling of comfort as I sat down to catch up with my reading and paper work. The peace of the night though urged me to ask why I had a sudden desire to question myself about the experience with Joy? The situation was like any other I had handled before but this time I was more prepared to ask for answers for the connectedness that I sensed so strongly. I was ready to examine my approach and sensitivities to an every day hospice event; I had to find out what this taught me that I felt was different.

There was pain that needed attention, Joy was in discomfort and was distrustful of my presence, as I was a stranger. Subconsciously I assessed the situation and acted on it. This was a first meeting between Joyce and myself. On reflection, I had recognised the critical perceptions of my actions and came to the conclusion that knowledge on multiple levels was what at the basis of handling this situation. In the dim night light meeting a complete stranger called on my abilities to 1) read the situation by being sensitive to Joyce's mood,[135] 2) analyse the environment, 3) close the personal distance[136] and replace the 'you and I' with 'I am you'.[137] This experience played an important role in making me aware of my capacity to understand and be truly present with Joyce's pain and suffering.[138] It also occurred to me that I had good symptom management skills that enabled me to perform the

---

135. JM Charon, *Symbolic Interactionism*, eighth edition (Upper Saddle River NJ: Pearson, 2004); PA Scott, PA 2000, 'Emotion, Moral Perception, And Nursing Practice', in *Nursing Philosophy*, 1 (2000): 123–133.
136. Maatta, 'Closeness And Distance In The Nurse-Patient Relations'.
137. H Spiro, 'What Is Empathy And Can It Be Taught?', in *Annals of Internal Medicine*, 116 (1992): 843–846.
138. P Willis, 'Looking For What It's Really Like: Phenomenology In Reflective Practice', in *Studies in Continuing Education*, 21/1 (1999); D Fingfeld-Connet, 'Meta-Synthesis Of Presence In Nursing', in *Journal of Advanced Nursing*, 55/6 (2006): 708–714; Covington, H 2005, 'Caring Presence: Providing A Safe Space For Patients', in *Holistic Nursing Practice*, 19/4 (2005): 169–172; P Authier, 'Being Present – The Choice That Re-Instills Caring, in *Nursing Administration Quarterly*, 28/4 (2004): 276–279; KL Melnechenko, 'To Make A Difference: Nursing Presence', in *Nursing Forum*, 38/2 (2003): 18-24.

right actions which led to the eventual beneficial outcome for Joyce in relieving her major symptom: pain.[139] This is palliative care at work.

---

139. SK Haworth and NM Dluhy, 'Holistic Symptom Management: Modelling The Interaction Phase', in *Journal of Advanced Nursing*, 36/2 (2001): 302–310; P Hill Bailey and S Tilley, 'Story Telling And The Interpretation Of Meaning In Qualitative Research', in *Journal of Advanced Nursing*, 38/6 (2002): 574–583; A Jablonski and KG Wyatt, 'A Model For Identifying Barriers To Effective Symptom Management At The End Of Life', in *Journal of Hospice and Palliative Nursing*, 7/1 (2005); S Brajtman, 'The Impact On The Family Of Terminal Restlessness And Its Management', in *Palliative Medicine*, 17 (2003): 454–460; EL Krakauer, RT Penson, RD Truog, LA King, BA Charner, and JR Lynch, 2000, 'Sedation For Intractable Distress Of A Dying Patient: Acute Palliative Care And The Principle Of Double Effect', in *The Oncologist*, 5 (2000): 53–62.

Bibliography

Aindow, A & Brook, L 2008, 'Essential medicines list for children', viewed 23.5.2012, http://www.who.int/selection_medicines/committees/subcommittee/2/palliative pdf

Agrimson, LB 2008, 'Spiritual crisis: a concept analysis', in *Journal of Advanced Nursing,* vol. 65, no. 2, pp. 454-461.

Alford, EF 2006, 'Only a piece of meat: one patient's reflection on her eight-day hospital visit', in *Qualitative Inquiry*, vol. 12, no. 3, pp. 596-620.

Anderson, L 2006,'Analytic autoethnography', in *Journal of Contemporary Ethnography,* vol. 35, no. 4, pp. 373-395.

Authier, P 2004, 'Being present – the choice that re-instills caring', in *Nursing Administration Quarterly*, vol. 28, no. 4, pp. 276-279.

Barbato-Gaydos, L 2004, 'The living end', in *Journal of Hospice and Palliative Care*, vol. 6, no.1, pp. 17-26.

Bartleet, BL 2009, 'Behind the baton: exploring autoethnographic writing in a musical context', in *Journal of Contemporary Ethnography,* vol. 38, no. 6, pp. 713-733.

Basset, C 2002, 'Nurses' perception of care and caring', in *International Journal of Nursing Practice,* vol. 8, no.1, pp. 8-15.

Bauby, JD 2000, *The diving bell and the butterfly,* Harper Perennial, London.

Behar, R 1996, *'The vulnerable observer'*, Beacon Press, Boston.

Benner, P 2001, *From novice to expert: excellence and power in clinical nursing practice,* Prentice Hall, Upper Saddler River, N.J.

Benner, P & Wruebel, J (eds) 1989, *The Primacy of caring,* Addison Wesley Publishing Company, Menlo Park, California.

Berger, L 2001, 'Inside out: narrative autoethnography as a path toward rapport', in *Qualitative Inquiry*, vol. 7, no. 4, pp. 504-518.

Berzoff, J & Silverman, PR (eds) 2004, *Living with dying: handbook for end-of-life healthcare practitioners,* Columbia University Press, New York.

Bochner, AP 1994, 'Perspectives on inquiry II', in *Handbook of Interpersonal Communication,* 2nd edn, (eds) ML Knapp & GR Miller, Sage Publications, Thousand Oaks, California.

Bochner, A 2001, 'Narrative Virtues', in *Qualitative Inquiry,* vol. 7, no. 2, pp. 131-158.

Bochner, AP 2007, 'Notes toward an ethics of memory in autoethnographic inquiry', in *Ethical Futures in Qualitative Research,* (eds) NK Denzin & MD Giardia, Left Coast Press Inc., Walnut Creek, CA94596.

Bochner, AP 2012, 'Suffering happiness', in *Qualitative Communication Research,* vol. 1, no. 2, pp. 209-229.

Bochner, AP & Ellis C1996, 'Introduction', in *Composing ethnography: alternative forms of qualitative writing,* (eds) C Ellis & AP Bochner, Alta Mira Press, Walnut Creek, California.

Bochner, AP & Ellis, C (eds) 2002, *Ethnographically Speaking: Autoethnography, Literature and Aesthetics,* Alta Mira Press, Walnut Creek, California.

Bolton, SC 2000, 'Who cares? offering emotion work as a "gift" in the nursing labour process', in *Journal of Advanced Nursing,* vol. 32, no. 3, pp. 580-6.

Bradshaw, A 1994, *Lighting the lamp: the spiritual dimensions of nursing care,* Scutari, London.

Bradshaw, A 1996, 'The spiritual dimension of hospice: the secularisation of an ideal', in *Social Science and Medicine,* vol. 43, no. 3, pp. 409-419.

Bradshaw, A 1999, 'The virtue of nursing: the covenant of care', *Journal of Medical Ethics,* vol. 25, no. 6, pp. 477- 481.

Bradshaw, A 2012, 'Gadamer's two Horizons: listening to the voices in nursing history', in *Nursing Inquiry,* vol. 195, no. 9, pp. 518-522.

Brajtman, S 2003, 'The impact on the family of terminal restlessness and its management', in *Palliative Medicine,* vol. 17, pp. 454-460.

Bruni, N 2002, 'Crisis of visibility: ethical dilemmas of autoethnographic research', in *Qualitative Research Journal,* vol 2, no. 1, pp. 24-32.

Buechner, F 1993, *Wishful thinking: a seeker's ABC,* Harper Collins Publishers, New York.

Buber, M 1958, *I and thou,* Charles Scribner's Sons, New York.

Buber, M 1998, *Knowledge of man: selected essays,* Educational Theory, Humanity Books, New York.

Burnard, P 2007, 'Seeing the psychiatrist: an autoethnographic account', in *Journal of research in nursing,* vol. 14, pp. 808-814.

Carper, BA 1978, 'Practice oriented theory: part 1, Fundamental patterns of knowing in nursing, *Advances in Nursing Science,* vol. 1 no. 1, pp. 13-23, in *Theoretical Nursing: Development and Progress,* 4th edn, AI Meleis, 2007.

Chalmers, David J (1995), 'Explaining consciousness: the "hard problem"', in *Journal of Consciousness Studies,* vol. 2, no. 3, pp. 200-219.

Chang, H 2008, *Autoethnography as method,* Left Coast Press, INC. 1630 North Main Street #400, Walnut Creek, CA 94596.

Charles, LL 2009, 'My nine lives as an academic: narratives of identity storied by a platinum-enhanced brain', in *Qualitative Inquiry,* vol. 15, no. 10, pp. 1592-1611.

Charmaz, K & Mitchell, RG Jnr 1997, 'The myth of silent authorship: self, substance, and style in ethnographic writing', in *Reflexivity and voice,* (ed) R. Hertz, Sage Publications, Thousand Oaks, California.

Charmaz, K 1999, 'Stories of suffering: subjective tales and research narratives', in *Qualitative Health Research,* vol. 9, no. 3, pp. 362-382.

Charon, JM 2004, *Symbolic Interactionism,* 8th edn, Pearson Prentis Hall, Upper Saddle River, New Jersey 07458.

Chase, SE 2001, 'Response to "The concept of nursing presence: state of the science"', in *Scholarly Inquiry for Nursing Practice: An International Journal,* vol. 15, pp. 323-327.

Chase, SE 2005, 'Narrative Inquiry' in *The Sage Handbook of Qualitative Research,* 3rd edn, (eds) NK Denzin & YS Lincoln, Sage Publications, Thousand Oaks, California.

Clarke, J 2006, 'A discussion paper about 'meaning' in the nursing literature on spirituality: an interpretation of meaning as 'ultimate concern' using the work of Paul Tillich', in *Nursing Studies,* vol. 43, pp. 915-921.

Clark, D 1996, 'Interview with Colin Murray Parkes', *Hospice History Program,* viewed on May 18, 2011, at 5.28 pm, http://www.hospice-history.org.uk

Clark D 2000, 'Total pain: the work of Cicely Saunders and the hospice movement', *APS Bulletin,* vol. 10, no. 4, viewed on 14.05.2011, http://www.ampainsoc.org/library/bulletin/jul00/hist.1.htm

Clark, D 2002, 'Between hope and acceptance: the medicalisation of dying', in *British Medical Journal,* vol. 324, no. 7342, pp. 905-907.

Clark, TW 2002, 'Is there an observing self?' *Science and Consciousness Review,* Viewed on 10.9. 2010, http://sciconrev.org/2004/02/is-there-an-observing-self

Coffey, A 1999, *The ethnographic self,* Sage Publications, London EC2A4PU.

Cohen, JB, 2004, 'Late for school: stories for transformation in an adult education program', in *Journal of Transformative Education,* vol. 2, no. 3, pp. 242-252.

Colaizzi, PF 1978, 'Psychological research as the phenomenologist views it', in *Existential-phenomenological alternatives for psychology,* (eds) RS Valle & M King, Oxford University Press, New York.

Coles, R 1989, *The call of stories: teaching and the moral imagination,* Boston: Houghton Mifflin.

Collins, M 1991, *Adult Education as Vocation,* Routledge, New York.

Covington, H 2005, 'Caring presence: providing a safe space for patients', in *Holistic Nursing Practice,* vol. 19, no. 4, pp. 169-172.

Cowling III, RW 1999, 'Unitary transformative nursing science: potentials for transcending dichotomies', in *Nursing Science Quarterly,* vol. 12, no. 2, pp. 132-137.

Cramer, LD, McCorkle, R, Cherlin, E, Johnson-Huzeler, R & Bradley, EH 2003, 'Nurses' attitudes and practice related to hospice care', in *Journal of Nursing Scholarship,* vol. 35, no. 3, pp. 249-255.

Cranton, P & Roy, M 2003, 'When the bottom falls out of the bucket', in *Journal of Transformative Education,* vol. 1, no. 2, pp. 86-98.

Cranton, P 2006, *Understanding and promoting transformative learning*, 2nd edn, Jossey-Bass, San Francisco CA.

Crawford, L 1996, Personal ethnography, in *Communication Monographs*, vol. 63, p. 158.

Dawson, J 2005, 'A history of vocation: tracing a keyword of work, meaning, and moral purpose', in *Adult Education Quarterly*, vol. 55, no. 3. pp. 220-231.

Denzin, NK 1992, 'The many faces of emotionality: reading persona', in *Investigating subjectivity*, (eds) C Ellis & MG Flaherty, Sage Publications, Newbury Park, London, New Delhi.

Denzin, NK 1999, 'Interpretive ethnography', vol. 28, no. 5, pp. 510-519.

Denzin, NK & Lincoln, YS (eds) 2000, *Handbook of Qualitative Research*, 2nd edn, Sage Publication, Thousand Oaks, California.

Denzin, NK & Lincoln, YS (eds) 2005, *The Sage Handbook of Qualitative Research*, 3rd edn, Sage Publications, Thousand Oaks, California.

Devine, A 2001, 'Narrating nursing jurisdiction: "atrocity stories" and "boundary work"', in *Symbolic Interaction*, vol. 24, no. 1, pp. 1-27.

Dik, BJ & Duffy, RD 2008, 'Calling and vocation at work: definition and prospects for research and practice', *The Counselling Psychologist*, vol. 37, no. 3, pp. 424-450.

Dobratz, M 1990, 'Hospice nursing: presence, perspectives and future directives', in *Cancer Nursing*, vol. 13, no. 2, pp. 16-22.

Dobratz, MC 2006, 'Enriching the portrait: methodological triangulation of life-closing theory', in *Advances in Nursing Science*, vol. 29, no. 3, pp. 260-270.

Dreyfus, H & Dreyfus, S 1986, *Mind over machine*, New York: Free Press.

Doyle, D, Hanks, G & MacDonald, N 2003, 'Introduction', in *The Oxford Textbook of Palliative Medicine*, 2nd edn, (eds) D. Doyle, G. Hanks & N. MacDonald, Oxford University Press, Oxford.

Duldt-Battey, BW 2004, 'Humanism, nursing, communication, and holistic care: a position paper on line, viewed 7.7.2011, http://www.samuelmerritt.edu/depts/nursing/duldt

DuBoulay, S 1984, *Cecily Saunders: Founder of the Modern Hospice Movement*, Hodder and Stoughton, London, Sydney, Auckland, Toronto.

Edvardsson, JD, Sandman, P & Rasmussen, BH 2003, 'Meaning of giving touch in the care of older patients: becoming a valuable person and professional', in *Journal of Clinical Nursing*, vol. 12, pp. 601-609.

Edvardsson, D & Street, A 2007, 'Sense or no-sense: the nurse as embodied ethnographer', in *International Journal of Nursing Practice*, vol. 13. pp. 24-32.

Edwards, SD 1998, 'The art of nursing', *Nursing Ethics*, vol. 5, no. 5, pp. 393-400.

Effken, JA 2007, 'The informational basis for nursing intuition: philosophical underpinnings', in *Nursing Philosophy*, vol. 8, pp. 187-200.

Eisen, MJ 2001, 'Peer-based professional development viewed through the lens of transformative learning', in *Holistic Nursing Practice*, vol. 16, no. 1, pp. 30-32.

Elias, D 1997, 'Its time to change our minds', *ReVision*, p. 26.

Elias, JI 2003, 'Reflections on the vocation of a religious teacher', in *Religious Education, The Official Journal of the Religious Education Association*, vol. 98, no. 3, pp. 297-310.

Elligson, L 1998, '"Then you know how I feel": Empathy, identification, and reflexivity in fieldwork', in *Qualitative Inquiry*, vol. 4, no. 4, pp. 492-514.

Elligson, LL 2006, 'Embodied knowledge: writing researchers' bodies into qualitative health research', in *Qualitative Health Research*, vol. 10, no. 2, pp. 298-310.

Ellis, C 1991, 'Sociological introspection and emotional experience', in *Symbolic Interaction*, vol.14, no. 1, pp. 23-50.

Ellis, C 2000,' Creating criteria: an ethnographic short story', in *Qualitative Inquiry*, vol. 6, no. 2, pp. 273-277.

Ellis, C 2001, 'Being real: moving towards social change', in *Qualitative Studies in Education*, vol. 13, no. 4, pp. 399-406.

Ellis, C 2004, '*The ethnographic I*', Alta Mira Press, Walnut Creek, Lanham, New York, Oxford.

Ellis, C 2007,'Telling secrets, revealing lives: relational ethics in research with intimate others', in *Qualitative Inquiry*, vol. 13, no. 1, pp. 1-14.

Ellis, C 2009, *Revision: autoethnographic reflections on life and work,* Left Coast Press Inc. 1630 North Main Street, #400 Walnut Creek, California 94596.

Ellis, C & Bochner, A 2000, Autoethnography, personal narrative, reflexivity, in *Handbook of Qualitative Research* 2nd edn, (eds) NK Denzin & YS Lincoln, Sage Publications, Thousand Oaks, California.

Ellis, C & Bochner, AP 2006, 'Analysing analytic autoethnography: an autopsy', in *Journal of Contemporary Ethnography, vol. 35, no. 4, pp. 429-449.*

Ellis, C & Flaherty, M (eds) 1992, *Investigating subjectivity: research on lived experience,* Sage Publications, Newbury Park, London, New Delhi.

Ellis, C, Kiesinger & Tillman-Healy, L 1997, 'Interactive interviewing: talking about emotional experience', in *Reflexivity and voice,* (ed) R Hertz, Sage Publications, Thousand Oaks, California.

Endo, E, Myahara, T, Suzuki, S & Ohmasa, T 2005, 'Partnering of researcher and practising nurses for transformative nursing', in *Nursing Science Quarterly,* vol. 18, no. 2, pp. 138-145.

Erikson, E 1987, 'The way of looking at things', in *Personality and personal growth,* 3rd edn, (eds) J Fadiman & R Frager, Harper Collins College Publishers, 10 East 53rd, Street, New York, 1994.

Estes, PC 1992, *'Women who run with the wolves',* Griffin Paperbacks, Watson Avenue, Netley, South Australia.

Etherington, K 2004, *Becoming a Reflexive Researcher,* Atheneum Press, Gateshead, Tyne and Wear.

Evans, JM & Hallet, CE 2007, 'Living with dying: a hermeneutic phenomenological study of the work of hospice nurses', in *Journal of Clinical Nursing,* vol. 16, pp. 742-751.

Fink, R & Gates, R 2006, 'Pain assessment' in *Textbook of palliative care,* 2nd edn, (eds) BR Ferrel & N Coyle, Oxford University Press.

Fingfeld-Connet, D 2006, 'Meta-synthesis of presence in nursing', in *Journal of Advanced Nursing,* vol. 55, no. 6, pp. 708-714.

Foster, K, McAllister, M & O'Brien, L 2006, 'Extending the boundaries: autoethnography as an emergent method in mental health nursing research', in *International Journal of Mental Health Nursing,* vol. 15, pp. 44-53.

Foster, E 2007, *Communicating at the end of life: finding magic in the mundane,* Lawrence Erlbaum Associates, Publishers, Mahwah, New Jersey, London.

Fredriksson, L 1999, 'Modes of relating in a caring conversation: a research synthesis on presence, touch and listening', in *Journal of Advanced Nursing,* vol. 30, no. 5, pp. 1167-1176.

Freshwater, D (ed) 2002, *Therapeutic Nursing,* Sage Publications, London, Thousand Oaks, New Delhi.

Frankl, V 1995, *Man's Search for Meaning,* Hodder and Stroughton, Seven Oaks California.

Gadamer, H.G 2000, *Truth and Method,* Continuum Publishing Company, New York.

Gadamer, H.G 1996, *Enigma of Health,* Stanford University Press, Stanford California.

Gastmans, C 1999, 'Care as a moral attitude', in *Nursing Ethics,* vol. 6, no. 3, pp. 214-223.

Gearity, BT & Mertz, N 2012, 'From "bitch" to "mentor": a doctoral student's story of self-change and mentoring', in *The Qualitative Report,* vol. 17, article 59, pp. 1-27, viewed 10 July 20, http://www.nova.edu/ssss/QR/QR17/gearity.pdf

Geertz, C 2000, *The interpretation of cultures,* Basic Books, New York.

Goodall, HL jnr. 2000, '*Writing the new ethnography*', Alta Mira Press, Walnut Creek, New York, Oxford.

Gordon, M 2011, 'Listening as embracing the other: Martin Buber's philosophy of dialogue', in *Educational Theory,* vol. 61, no. 2, pp. 207-219.

Guba, EG & Lincoln, YS 1994,' Competing paradigms in qualitative research', in *Handbook of qualitative research,* (eds) NK Denzin & YS Lincoln, Sage Publications, Thousand Oaks, California.

Gubrium, JF & Holstein, JA (eds) 1997, *The new language of qualitative method,* New York: Oxford University Press.

Gubrium, JF & Holstein, JA (eds) 2001, *"Handbook of Interview Research",* Sage Publications, Thousand Oaks, London, New Delhi.

Gubrium, JF & Holstein, JA (eds) 2003, *Postmodern interviewing,* Sage Publications, Thousand Oaks, California.

Hardy, S, Titchen, A & Manley, K 2007, 'Patient narratives in the investigation and development of nursing practice expertise: a potential for transformation', in *Nursing Inquiry,* vol. 14, no. 1, pp. 80-88.

Haworth, SK & Dluhy, N M 2001, 'Holistic symptom management: modelling the interaction phase', in *Journal of Advanced Nursing,* vol. 36, no. 2, pp. 302-310.

Hertz, R (ed) 1997, *Reflexivity and voice,* Sage Publications, Thousand Oaks, California 91320.

Hermann, CP 2001, 'Spiritual needs of dying patients: a qualitative study', in *Oncology nurses forum,* vol. 28, no 1.

Hill Bailey, P &Tilley, S 2002, 'Story telling and the interpretation of meaning in qualitative research', in *Journal of Advanced Nursing,* vol. 38, no. 6, pp. 574-583.

Holland-Wade, G 1998, 'A concept analysis of personal transformation', in *Journal of Advanced Nursing,* vol. 28, no. 4, p.713.

Holman-Jones, S 2005, 'Autoethnography: making the personal political' in *Handbook of Qualitative Research,* 3rd edn, (eds) NK Denzin & YS Lincoln, Sage Publications, Thousand Oaks, London, New Delhi.

Hopkinson, JB, Hallettt, CE & Luker, KA 2003, 'Caring for dying people in hospitals', in *Journal of Advanced Nursing,* vol. 44 no. 5, pp. 525.

Hospice Education Institute on line viewed 15.05.2011, http://www.hospiceworld.org/history.htm

Hupcey, JE, Penrod, J, Morse, JM & Mitcham, C 2001, 'An exploration and advancement of the concept of trust', in *Journal of Advanced Nursing,* vol. 36, no. 2, pp. 282-293.

Hutchings, D 1997, 'The hardiness of hospice nurses', in *The American Journal of Hospice and Palliative Care,* May-June, pp. 110-113.

Hutchinson, TA (ed) 2011, *Whole person care,* Springer, New York, Dordrec Heidelberg, London.

Jablonski, A & Wyatt, KG 2005, 'A model for identifying barriers to effective symptom management at the end of life', in *Journal of Hospice and Palliative Nursing,* vol. 7, no. 1.

Johns, C 2001.'Reflective practice: revealing the [he]art of caring', in *International Journal of Nursing Practice,* vol. 7, pp. 237-245.

Johns, C 2004, *'Being mindful, easing suffering, reflections on palliative care',* Jessica Kingsley Publishers, London and New York.

Johns, C 2006, 'Engaging reflection in practice', Blackwell Publishing, Oxford.

Johns, C 2010, Guided reflection: a narrative approach to advancing professional practice, Blackwell Publishing, Oxford.

Johns, C & Freshwater, (eds) 2005, Transforming nursing through reflective practice, 2nd edn, Blackwell Publishing, Oxford.

Johnston, B 2002, 'Overview of nursing developments in palliative care', in Palliative care: the nursing role, (eds) J Lugton & M Kidlen, Churchill Livingston.

Johnston, B & LN Smith 2005, 'Nurses and patients' perceptions of expert palliative nursing care' Journal of Advanced Nursing, vol. 54, no. 6, pp. 700-709.

Johnstone, MJ 1999, 'Reflective topical autobiography: an under utilized interpretive research in nursing', in Collegian, vol. 6, no. 1, pp. 24-29.

Kalmbach-Phillips, D, Harris, G, Legard-Larson, M & Higgins, K 2009, 'Trying on being: four women's journey(s) in feminist post-structural theory', in Qualitative Inquiry, vol. 15, pp. 1455-1479.

Kallstrom-Karlsson, IL, Ehnfors, M & Ternested, BM 2008, 'Five nurses' experiences of hospice care in a long-term perspective', in Journal of Hospice and Palliative Nursing, vol. 10, no. 4, pp. 224-232.

Kant, I 2007, Immanuel Kant: Critique of pure reason, trans. M Weigelt, Peguin, London.

Kehoe, MH 2006, ' Embodiment of hospice nurses: a meta-synthesis of qualitative studies', in Journal of Hospice and Palliative Nursing, vol. 8, no. 3, pp. 137-146.

Kendall, S 2007, 'Witnessing tragedy: nurses' perceptions of caring for patients with cancer', in International Journal of Nursing Practice, vol. 13, pp. 111-120.

Kidd, J & Finlayson, M 2009, 'When needs must: interpreting autoethnographical stories', in Qualitative Inquiry, vol.15, no. 6, pp. 34-50.

King, L & Appleton, JV 1997, 'Intuition: a critical review of the research and rhetoric', in Journal of Advanced Nursing, vol. 26, pp. 194-202.

King, C 2006, 'Nausea and vomiting', in Textbook of Palliative Nursing 2nd edn, (eds) BR Ferrel & N Coyle, Oxford University Press.

Kincheloe, JL & McLaren, P 2000, 'Rethinking critical theory and qualitative research, in *Handbook of Qualitative Research*, 2nd edn, (eds) NK Denzin & YS Lincoln, Sage Publications, Thousand Oaks, California.

Knight, K 2009, 'In his time of dying: communication and silence in family illness and death', in *Qualitative Inquiry*, vol. 15, no. 10, pp. 1612-1624.

Kobasa SC 1979, 'Stressful life events, personality and health: an inquiry into hardiness', in *Journal of Personal & Social Psychology*, vol. 37 pp. 34-37.

Kolker A 1996,'Thrown overboard: the human cost of health care rationing', in *Composing ethnography*, (eds) C Ellis & A Bochner, Alta Mira Press, Walnut Creek California.

Kottow, MH 2001, 'Between caring and curing', in *Nursing Philosophy*, vol. 2, pp. 53-61.

Kosowski, MM & Roberts, W 2003, 'When protocols are not enough: intuitive decision making by novice nurse practitioners', in *Journal of Holistic Nursing*, vol. 21, no. 1, pp. 52-72.

Krakauer, EL, Penson, RT, Truog, RD, King, LA, Charner, BA & Lynch, JR 2000, 'Sedation for intractable distress of a dying patient: acute palliative care and the principle of double effect', in *The Oncologist*, vol. 5, pp. 53-62.

Kunyk, D & Olson, JK 2001, 'Clarification and conceptualisation of empathy', in *Journal of Advanced Nursing*, vol. 35, no. 3, pp. 317-325.

Kubler-Ross, E 1969, *On death and dying*, Tavistock Publications, London.

Kvale, S 1996, *"InterViews"*, Sage Publications, Thousand Oaks, London, New Delhi.

Laskowski, C & Pellicore, K 2002, 'The wounded healer archetype: application to palliative care practice', in *American Journal of Hospice and Palliative Care*, vol. 19, no. 6, pp. 403-407.

Lavoie, M, Blondeau, D, & De Koninck 2008, 'The dying person: an existential being until the end of life', in *Nursing Philosophy*, vol. 9, pp. 89-97.

Liaschenko, J & Peter, E 2003,' Nursing ethics and conceptualisation of nursing: profession, practice and work', in *Journal of Advance Nursing*', vol. 46, no. 5, pp. 488-495.

Lindseth, A & Norberg, A 2004, 'A phenomenological hermeneutical method for researching lived experience', in *Scandinavian Journal of Caring Sciences,* vol. 18, pp. 145-153.

Linge, DE (ed) 1997, *Philosophical Hermeneutics-Hans Georg Gadamer,* University of California Press, Berkeley, Los Angeles, London.

Lundmark, M 2007, 'Vocation in theology-based nursing theories', in *Nursing Ethics,* vol. 14, no. 6, pp. 767-780.

Maatta, SM 2006, 'Closeness and distance in the nurse-patient relations: the relevance of Edith Stein's concept of empathy', in *Nursing Philosophy,* vol. 7, pp. 3-10.

Macnish, K 2002,' Palliative nursing', in *Palliative care for people with cancer,* 3rd edn, (eds) J Penson, & RA Fisher, Arnold Publishers, London, New York, New Delhi.

Magno, JB 2011, International Association for Hospice and Palliative Care, viewed at 11.06.2011, http://www.hospicecare.com/Bio/jb_magno.htm

Manias, E, Botti, M, Bucknall, M, 2002, 'Observation of pain assessment and management – the complexities of clinical practice', in *Journal of Clinical Practice,* vol. 11, pp. 724-733.

McCuthcheon, HH & Pincombe, J, 2001, 'Intuition: an important tool in the practice of nursing', in *Journal of Advanced Nursing,* vol. 35, no. 5, pp. 342-348.

Meleis, AI (ed) 2007, *Theoretical nursing,* 4th edn, Lippincot, Williams and Wilkins Publishers, Philadelphia.

Melnechenko, K.L 2003, 'To make a difference: nursing presence', in *Nursing Forum,* vol. 38, no. 2, pp. 18-24.

Mezirow, J 1991,*Transformative dimensions of learning,* Jossey-Bass, San Francisco.

Mezirow, J 1994, 'Understanding transformation theory', in *Adult Education Quarterly,* vol. 44, no. 4, pp. 222-232.

Mezirow, J (ed) 2000, *Learning as transformation,* Jossey-Bass, San Francisco.

Mezirow, J 2003, 'Transformative learning as discourse', in *Journal of transformative education,* vol. 1, no. 1, pp. 58-63.

Mintz, A 1978, *George Eliot & the novel on vocation,* Harvard University Press.

Mitchell, GJ 1999, 'The view of freedom within the human becoming theory', in *Illuminations,* (ed) R. Rizzo-Parse, Jones and Bartlett Publishers, Sudbury MA.

Mok, E & Chiu, PC, 2004, 'Nurse-patient relationship in palliative care', in *Journal of Advanced Nursing,* vol. 48, no. 5, pp. 475-483.

Muncey, T 2005, 'Doing autoethnography', in *International Journal of Qualitative Methods',* vol. 4, no. 1, pp. 2-1.

Muncey, T 2010, *Creating autoethnographies,* Sage Publications, Thousand Oaks, California.

Mykhalovskiy, E. 1997, 'Reconsidering "table talk": Critical thoughts on the relationship between sociology, autobiography and self-indulgence', in *Reflexivity and Voice,* (ed) R Hertz, Sage Publications, Thousand Oaks, London.

McAdams, DP 1993, *The stories we live by: personal myths and the making of the self,* Guilford Press, New York and London.

Newman, M 1994, *Health as expanding consciousness,* 2nd edn, Jones and Bartlet Publishers, Sudbury.

Newman, MA, Sime, MA & Corcoran-Perry, SA 1991,' The focus of the discipline of nursing', in *Advances in Nursing Science,* vol. 14, no. 1, pp. 1-6.

Newman, M, 2006, Health as Expanding Consciousness, Personal Web page, accessed 18.07.2007, http://www.healthexpandingconsciousness.org

Newman, MA 2008, *Transforming Presence,* F.A Davis Company, Philadelphia.

Nortvedt, P 1998, 'Sensitive judgment: an inquiry into the foundations of nursing ethics', in *Nursing Ethics,* vol. 5, no. 5, pp. 386-392.

Norris, JR 2002, 'One-to-one tele-apprenticeship as a means for nurses teaching and learning Parse's theory of human becoming', in *Nursing Science Quarterly,* vol. 15, no. 2, pp. 143-149.

O'Brien, ME 2001, *The Nurse's Calling,* Paulist Press, New York/Mahwah, N.J.

O'Hara, M 2002, 'Cultivating consciousness: Carl R. Rogers's person-centered group process as transformative androgogy', in *Journal of Transformative Education,* vol.1, no. 1, pp. 64-79.

Ohlen, J & Segesten, K 1997, 'The professional identity of the nurse: concept analysis and development', in *Journal of Advanced Nursing,* vol. 28, no. 4, pp. 720-727.

Ohman, M & Soderberg, S 2004, 'District nursing – sharing an understanding of being present. Experiences of encounters with people with serious chronic illness and their close relatives in their homes', in *Journal of Clinical Nursing*, vol. 13, pp. 858-855.

Olthuis, G, Dekkers, W, Leget, C & Vogelaar, P 2006, 'The caring relationship in hospice care: an analysis based on the ethics of caring conversations', in *Nursing Ethics*, vol. 13, no. 7, pp. 29-40.

O'Rawe-Amenta, M 1986, 'Holism, hospice and nursing', in *Nursing care of the terminally ill*, (eds) M O'Rawe-Amenta & NL Bohnet, Little, Brown and Company, Boston.

O'Rawe-Amenta, M & Bohnet, NL 1986, (eds) *Nursing Care of the Terminally Ill*, Little Brown and Company, Boston, Toronto.

Osmond, J & Darlington, Y 2005, 'Reflective analysis: techniques for facilitating reflection', in *Australian Social Work*, vol. 58, no. 1, pp. 3-14.

Panke, JT 2003,' Difficulties in managing pain at the end of life', *Journal of Hospice Nursing*, vol. 5, no. 3, pp. 83-90.

Parse, RR 1981, *Man-living-health: a theory of nursing*, John Wiley and Sons Publishers, New York, Chichester, Brisbane, Toronto.

Parse, RR (ed) 1999, *Illuminations: the human becoming theory in practice and research*, Jones and Bartlett Publishers, Sudbury.

Parse, RR 2002, 'The pattern that connects', *Advances in Nursing Science*, vol. 24, no. 3, pp. 1-7.

Parse, RR 2001, *Qualitative inquiry: the path of sciencing*, Jones and Bartlett Publishers, Sudbury.

Patton, JF 2006, 'Jungian spirituality: a developmental context for late-life growth', in *American Journal of Hospice and Palliative Medicine*, vol. 23, no. 4, pp. 304-308.

Payne, N 2001, ' Occupational stressors and coping as determinants of burnout in female hospice nurses', in *Journal of Advanced Nursing*, vol.33, no. 3, pp. 396-405.

Pesut, B 2008, 'A conversation on diverse perspectives of spirituality in nursing literature', *Nursing Philosophy*, vol. 9, pp. 98-109.

Pelias, RJ 2012, 'On the joy of connections', in *Qualitative Communication Research*, vol.1, no. 2, pp.163-167.

Perry, J 2001,' Dialogical intersection: the death of a father', in *Journal of Loss and Trauma*, pp. 161-182.

Petrosino, BM 1985, 'Characteristics of hospice patients, primary caregivers and nursing care problems: foundations for future research', in *The Hospice Journal*, vol. 1, pp. 3-9.

Picard, C & Jones, D 2005, *Giving voice to what we know*, Jones and Bartlett Publishers, Sudbury, Massachusetts.

Picard, C & Mariolis, T 2002, 'Praxis as a mirroring process: teaching psychiatric nursing grounded in Newman's health as expanding consciousness', in *Nursing Science Quarterly*, vol. 15, no. 2, pp. 118-122.

Polanyi, M 1966, *The tact dimension*, New York Garden: Garden City.

Poulos, CN 2008, 'Narrative conscience and the autoethnographic adventure: probing memories, secrets, shadows, and possibilities', in *Qualitative Inquiry*, vol. 14, no. 1, pp. 46-66.

Pratt, MB 1995, 'S/HE', Alyson Books, Los Angeles.

Pullman, D 2002, 'Human dignity and the ethics and aesthetics of pain and suffering', *Theoretical Medicine*, vol. 23, pp. 75-94.

Radwin, L & Alster, K 2002, 'Individualized nursing care: an empirical definition', in *International Nursing Review*, vol. 49, pp. 54-63.

Randall, F & Downey, R.S 2006, *Philosophy of Palliative Care*, Oxford University Press, Great Clarendon Street, Oxford.

Reed- Danahay, DE (ed) 1997, *Auto-Ethnography*, Berg Publishers, Oxford, New York.

Richardson, L 1992, 'The consequences of poetic representation: writing the other: rewriting the self', in *Investigating subjectivity: research on lived experience*, (eds) C Ellis & MG Flaherty, Sage Publications, Newbury Park, London, New Delhi.

Richardson, L 1997, *Fields of play: constructing an academic life*, Rutgers University Press, New Brunswick, New Jersey.

Riggio, RE & Taylor, S 2000, 'Personality and communication skills as predictors of hospice nurse performance', in *Journal of business and psychology*, vol. 15, no. 2, pp. 351-359.

Rogers, ME 1970, *The theoretical basis of nursing*, FA Davis Company, Philadelphia.

Rosenau, PM 1992, *Post-modernism and the social sciences*, Princeton University Press, Princeton, New Jersey.

Ruth-Sahd, LA & Tisdell EJ 2007, 'The meaning and use of intuition in novice nurses: a phenomenological study', in *Adult Education Quarterly*, vol. 57, no. 2, pp. 115-140.

Ryan, JJ 1977, 'Humanistic work: Its philosophical and cultural implications', in *A matter of dignity: Inquiries into the humanization of work*, (eds) W J Heisler & JW Houck, University of Notre Dame Press, Notre Dame.

Sabatino, CJ 1999, 'Reflections on the meaning of care', in *Nursing Ethics,* vol. 6, no. 5, pp. 574-582.

Sacks, JL & Nelson, JP 2007, 'A theory of non-physical suffering and trust in hospice patients', in *Qualitative Health Research,* vol. 17, no. 5, pp. 675-689.

Salamagne, M 1997, 'Hospice in France', in *Hospice care on the international scene,* (eds) C Saunders & R Kastenbaum, Springer Publishing Company Inc., New York.

Sandgren, A, Thulesius, H, Fridlund, B, & Petersson, K, 2006, 'Striving for emotional survival in palliative cancer nursing', in *Qualitative Health Research,* vol. 16, no. 1, pp. 79-95.

Sandstrom, KL, Martin, DD & Fine, GA (eds) 2006, *Symbols, selves and social reality,* 2nd edn, Roxbury Publishing Company, Los Angeles, California.

Saunders, C & Kastenbaum, R (eds) 1997, *Hospice care on the international scene,* Springer Publishing Company.

Saunders, C 1981, 'Hospices', in *Dictionary of Medical Ethics,* (eds) AS Duncan, CR Dunstan & RB Welbourne, Longman and Todd, London.

Schneider, P 2005, 'What does it take to be a good hospice nurse', Nevada Nurses Association, viewed on 05.06.2007, http://www.proquest.com

Scott, PA 2000, 'Emotion, moral perception, and nursing practice', in *Nursing Philosophy,* vol. 1, pp. 123-133.

Shaffir, W 1999,'Doing Ethnography: reflections on finding your way', in *Journal of Contemporary Ethnography,* vol. 28, no. 6, pp. 676-686.

Sherman-Heyl, B 2002, 'Ethnographic interviewing', in *Handbook of ethnography,* (eds) P Atkinson, A Coffey, S Delamont, J Lofland & L Lofland, Sage Publications Ltd, 6 Bonhill Street, London EC2a 4PU.

Shorter, M & Stayt, LC 2009, 'Critical care nurses experience of grief in an adult intensive care unit', in *Journal of Advanced Nursing,* vol. 66, no. 1, pp. 159-167.

Smith, C 2005, 'Epistemological intimacy: a move to autoethnography', in *International Journal of Qualitative Methods,* vol. 4. no. 2, pp. 1-7.

Sorensen-Marshall, E, 2009, 'Margaret Shanks, nurse to Susan B. Anthony: exploring the extraordinary in the "ordinary" nurse', in *Advances in Nursing Science,* vol. 32, no. 1, pp. 43-54.

Sorrell, JM 1994, 'Remembrance of things past through writing: aesthetic patterns of knowing in nursing', *Advances in Nursing Science*, vol. 17, no. 1, pp. 60-70.

Spiro, H 1992, 'What is empathy and can it be taught?', in *Annals of Internal Medicine,* vol. 116, pp. 843-846.

Spry, T 2011, 'Performative autoethnograph: critical embodiments and possibilities', in *The Sage Handbook of Qualitative Research,* 4th edn, (eds) NK Denzin & Y Lincoln, Sage Publications, Thousand Oaks, California.

Stanley, KJ 2002, 'The healing power of presence', in *Oncological Nurses Forum,* vol. 29, no. 6, pp. 935-940.

Strang, P, Strang, S, Hultborn, R & Arner, S 2004, 'Existential pain an entity, a provocation, or a challenge?', in *Journal of Pain and Symptom Management,* vol. 27, no. 3, pp. 241-250.

Sundin, K & Jansson, L 2003, 'Understanding and being understood as a creative caring phenomenon in care of patients with stroke and aphasia', in *Journal of Clinical Nursing*, vol. 12, pp. 107-116.

The Ottowa Citizen, April 25, 2005, 'A moral force: the story of Dr Balfour-Mount' on line, viewed on 18.05.11, http://www.canada.com/ottawacitizen/story.html?id=896d005a-fedd-4f50-fedd-a2d9-83a95fc56464

Teilhard de Chardin, P 2012, Quotation, viewed 14 January, 2011, http://www.brainyquote.com/quotes/authors/p/pierre_teilhard_de_chardi.htm#ixzz1jO1564pp

Thiel, MM & Harris, S 2005, 'Hope and vocation', in *The Journal of Supportive Oncology,* vol. 3, no.3, pp . 234-5.

Thoresen, L 2003, 'A reflection on Cicely Saunders' views on a good death through the philosophy of Charles Taylor', in *International Journal of Palliative Nursing,* vol. 9, no. 1, pp. 19-23.

Thornburg, P, Myers-Schim, S & Grubaugh, K 2008, 'Nurses' experiences of caring while letting go', in *Journal of Hospice and Palliative Nursing,* vol. 10, no. 6, pp. 382-391.

Tillman-Healy, L 1996, 'A Secret Life in Culture of Thinness: Reflection on Body, Food and Bulimia', in *Composing ethnography* (eds) C Ellis & A Bochner, Alta Mira Press, Walnut Creek, California.

Tillman, LM 2005, 'The State of Unions; Activism (and in-activism) in Decision 2004', Conference presentation, University of Chicago, Urbana Campus, 2005.

Vachon, ML 1987, *Occupational stress in the care of the critically ill, the dying and the bereaved*, Hemisphere Publishing Corporation, New York, Washington, Philadelphia, London.

Valle, RS & King, M 1978, *Existential-phenomenological alternatives for psychology*, Oxford University Press, New York.

Van Manen, M 1990, *Researching lived experience*, The University of Western Ontario, London, Ontario Canada.

Van Manen, M 1998, 'Modalities of body experience in illness and in health', *Qualitative Health Research*, vol. 8 no. 1, pp. 1-24.

Van Manen, M 1999, 'From meaning to method', in *Qualitative Health Research*, vol. 7, no. 3, pp. 345-369.

Warren, CAB, Archer D, Broderik SC, Dobbs D, Flores RF, Grow L, Hackney J, TX Garner, Kivett D, Johnson R, Pereira-Nunez ER & Robinson C 2000, 'Writing the other, inscribing the self', in *Qualitative Sociology*, vol. 2, no. 3, pp. 183-199.

Watson, J 1999, '*Postmodern nursing and beyond*', Churchill Livingston Harcourt Brace and Company Limited, 24-28 Oval Court, London NW 1 7DX.

Watson, J 2003, 'Love and caring: ethics of face and hand – an invitation to the heart and soul of nursing and our deep humanity', in *Nursing Administration Quarterly*, vol. 27, no. 3, pp. 197-202.

Wayman, LM & Barbato-Gaydos, HL 2005, 'Self-transcending through suffering', in *Journal of Hospice and Palliative Nursing*, vol. 7, no. 5, pp. 263-270.

Waymer, D 2008, 'A man: an autoethnographic analysis of black male identity negotiation', in *Qualitative Inquiry*, vol. 14 no. 6, pp. 968-989.

WebMD on line viewed 23.5.2012, http://www.webmd.com/search/search_results/default.aspx?query=Hospice

Weisman, AD 1977, 'The psychiatrist and the inexorable', in *New meanings of death*, (ed) H Feifel, McGraw-Hill, New York.

Wengstrom, Y & Ekedahl, M 2006, 'The art of professional development and caring in cancer nursing', in *Nursing and Health Sciences*, vol. 8, pp. 20-26.

White, SJ 1997, 'Empathy: a literature review and concept analysis", *Journal of Clinical Nursing*, vol. 6, pp. 253-25

White K 2002, 'Nursing as vocation', in *Nursing Ethics,* vol. 9, no. 3, p. 279.

White, S 2003, 'Autoethnography – an appropriate Methodology', in *Qualitative Research Journal,* vol. 3, no. 2, pp. 22-32.

Wilber, K 2004, *The Simple Feeling of Being,* Shambala Publication Inc.

Wilkinson, J 1999, 'Implementing reflective practice', in *Nursing Standard,* vol. 13, no. 21, pp. 36-41.

Willis, P 1999, 'Looking for what it's really like: phenomenology in reflective practice', *Studies in Continuing Education,* vol. 21, no. 1.

Wilson, C 2005, 'Said another way: My definition of nursing', in *Nursing forum,* vol. 40, no. 3, pp. 116-118.

World Health Organisation's definition of palliative care, on line, accessed 23.5.2012, http://whqlibdoc.who./hq/2003/WHO_CDS_STB_2003.22.pdf

World Health Organisation History, Projects, Structure 2012, on line, accessed 23.5.2012, http://en.wikipedia.org/wiki/World_Health_Organisation

Wright, DJ 2001, 'Hospice nursing: the speciality', in *Cancer Nursing,* vol. 24, no. 1, pp. 20-27.

Wright, DJ 2002, 'Researching the Qualities of Hospice Nurses', in *Journal of Hospice and Palliative Nursing,* vol. 4, no. 4. pp. 210-216.

Wright, J 2008, 'Searching one's self: the autoethnography of a nurse teacher', in *Journal of research in nursing,* vol. 13, no. 4, pp. 338-347.

York, L & Sharoff, L 2001, 'An extended epistemology for fostering transformative learning in holistic nursing education and practice', in *Holistic Nursing Practice,* vol. 16, no. 1, pp. 21-29.

Young, ML 2008, 'Death comes', in *Qualitative Inquiry,* vol. 14, no. 6, pp. 990-998.

Zikorus, P 2007, 'The importance of a nurse's presence', *Holistic Nursing Practice,* vol. 21, no. 4, pp. 208-210.

Zilberfein, F & Hurwitz, E 2004, 'Clinical social practice at the end of life', in *Living with Dying,* (eds) J Berzoff & PR Silverman, Columbia University Press, New York.

Zysberg, L & Berry, MD 2005, 'Gender and students' vocational choices in entering the field of nursing', in *Nursing Outlook,* vol. 53, pp. 193-198.